CONTENTS

GW00600645

INTRODUCTION

This is not a cookery book! It is an eclectic mix of my favourite recipes, chosen as much for their 'Fat boy' appeal as their originality. Many are traditional English, some spicy. Most are simple and easy to prepare but all, I hope, are delicious to eat.

I make no pretence of being a professional cook or solipsistic dietician. I simply love food, eating as well as preparing it and I have chosen to write this book, as most recipe books I have read seem always to be written for slim, diet conscious people. I haven't found one yet that caters for fat, heavy drinking males.

These recipes are what in old English were called receipts, as in Edward Kidder's '*Receipts of Pastry and Cookery For The Use of his Scholars*', written around 1720. They are not written in stone and are meant only as a guide to aid the preparation of dishes.

It is claimed that the English understand little about food; that we have few national dishes of merit and are willing to accept poor quality and standards in our restaurants. Today, this of course, is rubbish.

The records of English recipes dating back to around 1280 contain a dazzling array of spices from all over the world. They include saffron, ginger, pepper, almonds, as well as sugar from North Africa. (1). The recipes themselves appear to owe more to the style of cooking in the Eastern Mediterranean and North Africa than to Western Europe. They suggest a sophistication of gastronomic excellence rarely seen in Europe since. Many of those early English recipes do not appear in French books of the period. However, there is a closer relationship with recipes of the period found in Italy and Spain, which countries were influenced more by Persian and Arabian cookery.

The Romans introduced geese, pheasant, guinea fowl and rabbits to this country, as well as spices such as white mustard, chervil, dill, coriander and parsley. They also introduced peach, almond, cherry, quince and medlar trees, to England.

In the Middle Ages, royal dinners in England included dishes such as 'Mawmenny' (which became our blancmange), consisting of minced pork or chicken poached in wine and flavoured with cloves and thickened with ground almonds; 'Hausgeme', which was a mixture of diced and minced veal simmered in almond milk, flavoured with galingal, cinnamon and sugar and thickened with rice flour. Sauces, too, were highly sophisticated. 'Bukkenade' was a meat sauce made from pounded veal and meat broth with herbs and spices, thickened with egg yolks and sharpened with verjuice (made from unripe grapes), to be served with goat, veal, chicken or rabbit. They had ginger sauce for lamb and suckling pig; camelyn sauce, made from ground currants and walnuts, cinnamon and breadcrumbs and vinegar, for eating with heron, crane, plover and bustard. Also, a more familiar green sauce made from mint, parsley, garlic, sage and thyme with vinegar and breadcrumbs which was eaten with fish. These are not the recipes of a greedy roast beef-eating race of tasteless Philistines. (2)

From the 16th to the 19th centuries we were renowned throughout Europe for the quality, variety and quantity of the food we served. In England feasting became so out of control at banquets that by 1517, the King was forced to introduce legislation to restrict the number of courses to three for rich citizens with an annual income of over £500, six for peers and nine for cardinals. (3) (Could you see our, sybaritic, control-freak, politically correct Government getting away with that sort of legislation today?)

Roasted and boiled meats of all kinds were served in the taverns and grand houses all over the country and a visiting French traveller in 1690 wrote that as many as ten meat courses followed by fish, pies and puddings were the norm. Peasants he saw as he travelled around the country were better dressed and shod in comparison to those in France and the food they ate was richer and more varied. Over twenty cookery books were published in England between 1500 and 1600 but in France, only one, Viandier which ran to fifteen editions.

Appreciation of English cooking is changing. In the 1960's we witnessed the arrival and subsequent decline in popularity of Nouvelle Cuisine from France – that self-appointed denizen of epicurean style. Since then, we have seen the steady growth in popularity here of Chinese, Indian, West Indian, Spanish, Italian, Japanese and Thai food. The quality of which is far superior in restaurants in this country than any other. This may be because we take little pride in our domestic culinary traditions or simply because we are happy to welcome new ideas about food with open arms. Specialist shops selling raw ingredients from all over the World are common now in most towns across the Country. Where in Paris can you find a good curry house or a quality sushi bar? The choice of dishes in restaurants in Venice is about as broad as that found in a small midlands town, although a lot more expensive, and from a culinary point of view, the city is about as exciting as Cardiff.

We appear to have forgotten our own strengths and continue to labour under the misguided belief that we have little to offer in the way of good traditional English food. This inferiority complex is beginning to change and the change is long overdue. Regardless of what the French claim, we still produce the finest beef and lamb in Europe.

This recipe collection, I hope, may provide like-minded people with a few ideas. I have ignored the rules of calorific control, which I consider a total waste of time and calories themselves no more than an invention of ambitious American health freaks.

Friends have kindly sent me a selection of their favourite recipes and some ideas have been gleaned from old newspaper articles over the years, sampled and amended. I do not claim much in the way of original thought as far as these ideas are concerned. I do, however, believe that only by experimenting is it possible to get real pleasure from the cooking experience. It doesn't matter where you get the idea – it is what you do with it that is important. I abhor those professional cooks who try to create mystery out of what is, after all, a very basic skill. I also do my best to slap down the foodie commentators who try hard to dictate what food goes with what and who lecture us on avoiding this and that technique or style of cooking. To hell with them all! Experiment as you wish. I remember reading an article, written by some pompous cook for a local newspaper, declaring that fish and meat should never be consumed together because the taste of one kills the flavour of the other. What absolute rubbish. There is nothing in the world better than a plate of barbecued lobster tail and rib-eye steak!

There are two important rules when using these recipes. Please read them all the way through before you start! I may have got the ingredients out of order. The second is always to remember that it is important to adjust the quantities to suit your personal taste. The recipes are designed as a guide with which to experiment. After all that is what this is all about!

(1) *Cane sugar first appeared in the Royal Rolls in 1205.*
(2) *More detail of what was eaten in those days can by read in Colin Spencer's excellent book British Food – An Extraordinary Thousand Years of History (Grub Street 2202).*
(3) *Roy Strong, Feast, p. 104 and 146.*

Squire Mytton

'Mad' Jack Mytton, born at Halston near Oswestry in 1796, was a famous Shropshire Squire whose love of fine wine and feasting was legendary. He would qualify today as a perfect example of a 'Fat boy' gourmand. His father died when he was an infant and after he came of age, he inherited the Halston estate and a £70,000 fortune, a great sum in those days. His house parties lasted for days and his wife was never sure how many of his many friends would turn up with him after a day's hunting or from the races, expecting to be fed. He had a prodigious appetite and was known to consume up to 8 bottles of port a day. He died penniless in 1834, aged 38, the most popular squire in Shropshire. Fourteen thousand people, both rich and poor, lined the road from Shrewsbury to Halston, a fifteen-mile route, to watch his cortege pass. Church bells tolled and every shop in town was closed.

His many deeds of kindness will never be forgotten and all those who had known him gathered to bid farewell to a popular hedonist, the likes of which we will probably never see again.

CHAPTER ONE

SOUPS

Soup can be a meal in itself and it would be unfortunate if it always featured as a starter. We enjoy hearty vegetable soups in the winter which contain some or all the vegetables we have growing in the garden or left over from other meals. Here, I have included a selection of soups that are easy to make and full of flavour.

Marianne's Prawn Shell Soup

Try saying that after a sherbet or two! First buy a load of cooked prawns and eat them with home-made mayonnaise. Instead of throwing out the discarded shells, follow the instructions below. The result is one of the finest soups I have ever tasted when served chilled in small coffee cups.

To serve 2 with the prawns and 4 people with the soup

1 pint boiled prawns (1 lb)

1 onion, finely chopped

1 celery stalk, chopped

1 oz. butter

1 tbsp. tomato ketchup and/or

2 tsp. tomato puree

1 tin of tomatoes

2 glasses white wine or dry sherry

1 pint chicken or fish stock

1 cup double cream

1/2 tsp. cayenne pepper

Salt & pepper

Method

First eat the prawns and save the shells. In a pan, fry the onion in the butter until it softens, add the prawn shells and celery and continue to stir-fry for a few more minutes. Add the stock and all other ingredients except the cream and simmer for half an hour on low heat. Do not boil. Remove from the heat, allow to cool and then puree in a blender. Sieve, reheat and add the cream and season with salt and pepper. Serve hot or chilled in small coffee cups. The result should be a rich, creamy, highly concentrated fish soup.

French Canadian Onion Soup
(Gratinee)

I think the Canadian version of this soup is close to the original 18th century French recipe. Great 'Fat boy' winter food! 'Gratin' is French for the crust that forms on top of the soup, created by melting cheese or eggs and breadcrumbs. 'Gratinee' is a Parisian speciality, traditionally served for late supper in the bistros of Montmartre.

To serve 4

4 large onions

2 tsp. sugar

1 3/4 pints beef stock

1/4 pint dry white wine

3 egg yolks

4 tbsp. butter

5 fl. oz. Madeira or port

3 crushed cloves garlic

1 oz. flour

6 slices French bread

Grated Canadian Cheddar cheese or Gruyere

Salt & freshly ground black pepper and nutmeg

Method

Slice the onions very thinly and fry them gently in most of the butter and sugar until they begin to caramelize and turn golden. Sprinkle with the flour and continue to fry, stirring regularly until brown, then add the beef stock and white wine. Bring to the boil, stirring constantly and reduce. Remove to lower heat and add the garlic and simmer for at least an hour to allow the flavours to merge.

In the meantime, dry the slices of bread in the bottom oven of the Aga or slow oven. When the onion soup is cooked, mix the egg yolks with the Madeira and stir into the soup. Season with salt, pepper and nutmeg and pour the soup into individual bowls. Butter each slice of bread and sprinkle with a generous helping of grated cheese and float the bread on top of the soup. Place the bowls in a bain-marie. Pour boiling water into the baine-marie, up to halfway up the bowls and cook in a hot oven until the top of the bread is well browned. Serve immediately, piping hot!

Clam Chowder

Again, we prefer the Canadian version of this satisfying soup, which we found in Nova Scotia. It takes some time to prepare the live shellfish but it is well worth the effort. Should you be short of time, tinned shellfish would do but the flavour will never be the same.

To serve 6 or 8

2 lbs clams

1 lb mixture of live (in their shells) scallops, mussels and a few oysters

1 glass dry white wine

8 oz. cod fillets

1 pint milk

1 onion finely chopped

4 oz. butter

1 garlic clove finely chopped

1 potato, diced

4 thick slices unsmoked streaky bacon or pancetta, diced

Fresh sprig of thyme

1/4 pint fresh cream

Salt and pepper

Method

Clean the shells, removing any beards from the mussels. Put the clams and mussels in a pan with half the wine and cook on high until the shells open, after about 5 minutes. Discard any that remain closed. Place the oysters and scallops in a roasting tin with the rest of the wine and bake in the oven for a few minutes until the shells open, Again discarding any that remain closed. Shuck all the shellfish and discard the shells. Remove and discard the intestinal sac and remove the coral from the scallops. Keep the juice the shellfish was cooked in and the rejected coral and boil. When well reduced, strain and put aside. Simmer the potatoes in the milk with the thyme until soft. Fry the diced bacon in a little butter. When browned, remove from the pan and set aside. Fry the onion and garlic in the rest of the butter until well browned. Cube the fish fillets and poach in the milk for 2 or 3 minutes. Combine the potatoes, milk, fish, bacon and onions together with the juices from the frying pan and some of the cooking liquid and heat gently. Before it reaches boiling point remove from the heat, stir in the cream and check the seasoning. The chowder should be served warm with crackers or fresh French bread and a good dry white wine.

Mulligatawny Soup
(Kerala, South India)

Soup does not form part of a traditional Indian meal and mulligatawny, Tamil for pepper-water, (molagu meaning pepper and thanni meaning water) was introduced by Officers of the Raj as an appetiser before dinner. Ultimately, it became popular as a light lunch, particularly in South India. The soup was served piping hot into large soup bowls and a steaming bowl of boiled rice was passed around the table.

If the rice was cooked in the soup, it became extremely glutinous and mushy but when added later, it made a most delicious and filling meal.

To make soup for 4 people
For the spice paste

1 tsp. freshly grated nutmeg

1 tbsp. freshly ground coriander

1 tsp. freshly ground cumin

1 tsp. turmeric powder

3 hot red chillies, finely chopped

6 ground cloves

3 cloves garlic, crushed

6 ground black peppercorns

1 inch ginger root, grated

For the rest

1 onion, finely chopped

Butter for frying

1 lb minced lamb

2 pints meat stock

1 carrot, finely chopped

1 apple, finely chopped

Salt and pepper

Method

Blend the spices into a smooth paste. Fry the onion in some butter until soft and add the paste. Cook for a while in a heavy pot. Add the lamb and cook, stirring all time, for 5 or 6 minutes until well browned. Add the stock, salt and pepper and bring to the boil. Lower heat and simmer for half an hour or until meat is tender. Add the carrot and apple and continue to simmer. When cooked, mash the carrot and apple into the soup and serve with boiled rice. The resultant soup should be thick, spicy and hot.

Coconut Soup with Poached Eggs

I am not sure if this rates as a soup or a way of poaching eggs but it is based on a dish favoured in Kerala and it goes well with a curry or, indeed, as a starter for any meal.

To serve 4

4 eggs

1 onion, finely sliced

1 tomato, finely chopped

1 Thai chilli, deseeded and chopped

$1/2$ packet creamed coconut, dissolved in 1 pint water

$1/2$ tsp. each freshly ground cumin, coriander, and turmeric

Juice of one lemon

Butter and oil for frying

Salt & pepper

Method

Heat the oil and butter in a pan and fry the onions until they soften and begin to turn brown. Add the powdered spices and the chopped chilli and stir-fry for a few minutes to release the flavours. Add the chopped tomato and fry for a further few minutes until the tomato begins to melt. Add the coconut cream, season, stir and bring to the boil. Simmer for a few minutes until the mixture thickens slightly then, if you are ready to serve the soup immediately, gently break the eggs into the soup, cook for about 3 or 4 minutes and serve in separate bowls, ensuring that each bowl gets one egg. Should you decide to wait before serving the soup, keep the soup warm until it is required then heat to boiling and follow the instructions above.

Ham & Vegetable Soup
(Harira)

This soup is served during Ramadan in Morocco and is renowned for being fortifying and satisfying at the end of a hard day's work.

To serve 4 – 6

$1/4$ pint vegetable oil

4 sliced onions

8 oz. ham, cut into $1/2$ inch cubes

6 tomatoes, peeled and chopped

2 handfuls parsley, roughly chopped

1 tsp. each powdered ginger, paprika, black pepper, cumin, salt and turmeric

3 carrots, chopped

2 quarts water

2 marrow bones if possible or
2 Oxo cubes

$1/2$ lb chickpeas, soaked overnight

$1/4$ lb dried beans or lentils

$1/4$ lb rice and/or vermicelli

4 eggs

Method

Heat the oil in a large pot until smoking, add the onions and meat and fry until browned all over. Add the tomatoes, parsley, spices and vegetables. Stir to allow the spices to release their aroma and add the water, marrowbones or Oxo cubes dissolved in a little of the water. Bring to the boil and simmer for an hour or more. Add the chickpeas and beans and continue to cook, stirring frequently. Half an hour before it is to be served add the rice and vermicelli and about 10 minutes before it is ready, add the eggs from the shells and quickly stir so that the strands of egg white can be seen in the soup.

Ham & Shrimp Soup
(Sopa de Quarto de Hora)

This Spanish soup does indeed take no longer than quarter of an hour to make, hence the name. It is filling, easy to prepare and flexible as far as ingredients are concerned and, more particularly, very tasty.

To serve 4

1 1/2 – 2 pints well-seasoned fish stock

1/2 cup rice

1/2 cup peeled shrimps or prawns (either cooked or raw)

2 hard-boiled eggs chopped fine

1/2 lb Serrano diced (any ham or boiled bacon will do)

Salt & pepper

Method

Boil the stock and add the rice. After about 5 or 10 minutes add the shrimps, chopped egg and ham and simmer on medium heat until the rice is cooked. Season and serve. Simple! The result should be thick, hearty soup rather like a runny risotto.

Tony's Garlic Soup

Believe me, this is a good hangover cure. The garlic smell disappears but the goodness remains. The result should be a smooth, creamy and delicately flavoured soup, best served with fingers of buttered toast. Simple!

To serve 4

2 egg yolks

Good quality olive oil

2 large whole garlic bulbs

1 pint water

Salt & pepper

Method

Make some mayonnaise with the egg yolks and sufficient oil, season with salt and pepper and pour it into an ovenproof soup tureen. Crush the garlic and put it, skins and all, to boil in the lightly salted water for 45 minutes or so. Strain the garlic-flavoured liquid onto the mayonnaise in the tureen a little at a time, stirring vigorously. Mash the skinned garlic into a paste and add to the liquid. Strain, whisk to froth and serve hot in small bowls with buttered toast fingers.

Vegetable and Herb Soup

This simple soup, described as "light, fresh and full of flavour" was contributed by Michael Caines, head chef and director of Gidleigh Park Hotel, near Chagford. He suggested trying different herbs to experiment with flavours but advised using only fresh herbs, to be added to the pot at the last moment. The size of the vegetable dice doesn't have to be exact but it is important that they are all cut to the same size to ensure the vegetables are evenly cooked.

To serve 4

1 oz. shallots, finely chopped

1 1/2 oz. leeks finely sliced

2 oz. each carrots, courgettes, celeriac, chopped into 1/2 inch sq. dice

2 oz. cabbage, shredded and chopped into 1/2 inch pieces

2 oz. peas

2 oz. French beans chopped into 1/2 inch sq. dice

2 oz. tomato, blanched, skinned and seeded, chopped into 1/2 inch sq. dice

2 fl. oz. white wine

1 pint each, chicken stock and water

12 basil leaves, roughly chopped

1 tsp. each, chervil, chives and sorrel, roughly chopped

3 fl. oz. cream

5 oz. unsalted butter

Pinch of sugar

Salt & pepper

Method

Sweat the shallots, leeks, celeriac and carrot in 1 oz. of butter with a pinch of salt for about five minutes to colour. Add the wine and reduce to nothing. Add the water and chicken stock and bring to the boil. Continue to boil for about 10 minutes, then add the courgettes, French beans, peas and cabbage and simmer for a further 5 minutes. Remove from the heat, add the cream and whisk in the butter, add the herbs and chopped tomato, season with salt and pepper and a pinch of sugar.

Beef Soup with Dumplings

I am told this soup originated in the West Indies. It is both filling and loaded with flavour.

To serve 6
For the soup

1 lb stewing beef, diced into small pieces

1 onion, finely sliced

1 carrot, chopped

1 sweet potato, peeled and cut into chunks

1 small turnip, peeled and cut into chunks

7 oz. ladies' fingers (okra)

2 hot chillies, deseeded and chopped

1 pint chicken stock

1 tin coconut milk

1 tbsp. coriander seeds

Olive oil for frying

Salt & freshly ground black pepper

For the dumplings

3 tbsp. self-raising flour

3 tbsp. plain white flour

2 oz. lightly salted butter

Salt and freshly ground black pepper

Method

Mix the dumpling ingredients together, adding sufficient water to form a stiff dough. Form into table tennis sized balls and set aside.

Fry the meat in the olive oil until it is well browned. Add the sliced onions, carrots, sweet potato, chilli and coriander seeds and cook, covered, on a low heat for half an hour. Add the chicken stock and the dumplings and continue to cook, covered, on low heat for a further half-hour. Add the coconut milk and ladies' fingers and cook for a further 15 minutes. Season and serve.

Minestrone

Like so much peasant cooking in Italy there are more ways of preparing minestrone than there are days in the year. The ingredients change with the season as well as the district in which it is made. This one makes a sound 'Fat boy' winter soup that is hard to beat.

To serve 6

1 small cabbage or half a large one, roughly chopped

4 rashers of smoked bacon, roughly chopped

2 each carrots and leeks, peeled, quartered lengthways and chopped

4 sticks celery, peeled, quartered and chopped

2 14 oz. tins chopped plum tomatoes

2 onions, finely chopped

5 cloves garlic, sliced

7 oz. spaghetti sticks

1 $1/2$ pints chicken stock

Extra virgin olive oil

A couple of handfuls basil

1 tbsp. fresh rosemary

Salt & freshly ground black pepper

Handful grated Parmesan cheese

Method

Put some olive oil in a heavy pan and fry the bacon. Add the onions, carrots, celery, leeks, garlic and rosemary and sweat for 20 minutes or so until all is tender. Add the chopped tomato and stock and bring to the boil. Simmer for 10 minutes and then add the cabbage and simmer, covered for a further 10 minutes. Then break the spaghetti into $1/4$ inch lengths and add to the soup and stir gently for a further 5 minutes. Check seasoning and serve in deep bowls with a swirl of olive oil and some grated Parmesan cheese on the top.

Dr William Buckland

"I always maintained that the taste of mole was the most repulsive I knew – until I tasted a bluebottle" said Dr William Buckland, Dean of Westminster, an eccentric gourmet. He would eat almost anything that moved including hedgehog and crocodile steak – crocodile is apparently very tough indeed. His son, however, born in 1826, far exceeded his father in his eccentric eating habits. Elephant's trunk soup was one that didn't last long on his menu but he did try panther meat and mice fried in batter and many other delicacies.

He kept a large collection of stuffed animals around his house as well as dead meat in his larder waiting to be cooked. On one occasion a female guest tripped over a stuffed animal on the stairs as she climbed in the dark. Instead of being sympathetic he reprimanded her for her carelessness. "Hippopotami do not grow on trees", he told her sharply!

CHAPTER TWO

FISH

It is a shame these days that we seem to get such poor quality fish in this country. We are surrounded by sea and yet are told how desperate the fishermen are to make a living. Due largely to the extraordinary rules of the European Community, however, fish stocks are depleting rapidly. Why have all the wet fishmongers given up and why is it possible to buy so much better fish in France at a cheaper price?

As a family we adore fish and will happily eat it raw as in sushi, smoked, pickled, barbecued, grilled or poached, but the sadness is, we now think of it as a seasonal treat rather than regular fare.

The dampness of the British climate led the Romans to seek other ways of preserving fish here, rather than the more accepted method of wind drying favoured in the warmer, southern parts of Europe. As a result, salting, became the favoured means of providing sea-caught fish to inland towns and communities. By the fourteenth century, however, the smoking of fish, such as herring, salmon and trout became popular throughout England.

Smoked Fish Pie

This is an excellent, easy and filling recipe for a winter's night supper party. It is best prepared with undyed smoked haddock and it does no harm to throw in a chopped slice or two of other smoked fish, salmon or trout maybe.

To serve 6

2 lbs smoked haddock

10 fl. oz. full cream milk

1 lb potatoes

2 large onions, chopped

2 hard boiled eggs, roughly chopped

2 oz. Cheddar cheese, grated

1 handful, white bread crumbs

1 tbsp. plain flour

2 oz. butter

Salt & freshly ground black pepper

Method

Parboil the potatoes in salted water until they are nearly tender, allow to cool, then peel and slice them. Poach the fish in milk for 2 or 3 minutes and lift it out with a slotted spoon. When cool enough to handle, remove the skin and all the bones and flake the fish into a buttered ovenproof dish. Fry the chopped onions in some of the butter until they become soft and translucent. Remove them with the slotted spoon and add to the fish. Stir in the flour with the rest of the butter and gradually add the poaching liquid, stirring constantly, season well to make a creamy sauce. Add the chopped eggs to the dish, gently mix everything together and pour over half the sauce. Top with the potato slices, cover with the remainder of the sauce and scatter the grated cheese and breadcrumbs over the top. Bake in a hot oven for 20 minutes or until the topping turns light brown. Serve with spring greens and grilled tomatoes.

Kedgeree
(Khichri)

Kedgeree is one of several dishes which, over the years, have found their way from India in the days of the Raj. In its traditional Indian form it is called khichri, a vegetarian comfort food consisting of a mix of boiled rice, lentils and fried vegetables, usually onions. It is not clear why and when lentils were replaced by smoked fish and hard-boiled eggs, but there is no doubt it has become a common and welcome English breakfast staple.

As an alternative, smoked salmon, even smoked herring or mackerel can replace the haddock and also, fried onions rather than parsley can be sprinkled on top. Should you decide to stick to haddock, avoid using the darker artificially smoked fish. Serve at breakfast or as a light supper with Tabasco and tomato sauce.

To serve 4

1 lb boiled Basmati rice

8 oz smoked haddock fillet, poached in milk

2 tbsp. butter

2 hard-boiled eggs, roughly chopped

8 fl. oz. double cream

1 raw egg

$1/2$ tsp. grated nutmeg

1 tsp. each turmeric powder, ground cumin and grated ginger

1 or 2 hot green chillies, cut into fine strips to taste

Salt and pepper

Method

Flake the fish and ensure all bones are removed. Melt the butter in a large frying pan, add the cooked rice, flaked fish, turmeric powder, cumin, ginger and roughly chopped eggs. Toss gently until hot and add the cream, grated nutmeg and chilli shreds and stir. Make a hole in the centre of the rice and break in the egg, cover with rice and leave to cook for a moment or two and then stir the egg through the rice to encourage it into shreds. Serve hot, with some parsley or fried onion rings sprinkled on top.

Salmon Fishcakes on Spinach

Rather like lamb cutlets, this is a dish commonly found in West End Clubs, old-fashioned restaurants in Brighton and other seaside resorts, or school canteens. They may appear rather ordinary but, if done properly, they are 'truly historic' as one food commentator is noted for saying!

To serve 6 or 4 greedy ones

1 $1/2$ lb salmon fillet, skinned

1 $1/2$ lb mashed potato

3 anchovy fillets, mashed to a paste

2 tbsp. tomato ketchup or tomato puree

2 tbsp. Coleman's mustard

2 tsp. Worcestershire sauce

Flour and butter for frying

2 lb spinach, washed and cleaned

Salt & freshly ground black pepper

Method

Poach the salmon in fish stock if available, if not, dissolve a chicken stock cube in enough water instead. When the fish has been lightly cooked, remove from the stock and flake. Mix together until smooth the potato, half the flaked salmon, ketchup, mustard and anchovy paste and season well. Gently fold in the rest of the salmon flakes and mould the mixture into as many flat round cakes as required. Place all the cakes in the fridge, covered with clingfilm, for at least an hour. Lightly flour the fishcakes and fry them in the butter until they are browned on both sides. Keep the cakes warm whilst you prepare the spinach. Put the spinach in a saucepan with the minimum of water, season and cook for about 3 minutes until the leaves are tender. Drain. Place a portion of spinach in the centre of each plate, place a fishcake on top and serve with homemade tomato ketchup.

Salt Cod
(Bacalhau)

Salt cod, in Devon parlance, was known as 'toe rag' because the farmers thought the stink unbearable. However, if soaked properly and cooked as in this adapted Portuguese recipe, the result is delicious.

To serve 4

1 $1/2$ lb dried salt cod

2 onions, finely sliced

Olive oil

1 lb potatoes, boiled and sliced

3 eggs, hard boiled and roughly chopped

4 cloves garlic, crushed

2 oz. black olives, stoned

Handful chopped parsley

Freshly ground black pepper & salt
(The dish will be unlikely to require much salt but try a flake of fish to check before adding any)

Method

Soak the cod in cold water for at least 24 hours or longer, if needed, with frequent changes of water. Simmer in just enough water to cover for 2 or 3 hours until the fish is tender. Remove the skin and carefully flake the fish into large pieces, removing all bones and set aside. Fry the onions in oil in an oven-proof casserole until soft. Add the potatoes, cod, garlic and olives. Drizzle some olive oil over the top with a knob of butter and season with black pepper. Bake in a moderate oven for about 10 minutes. Serve, garnished with the chopped egg and parsley straight from the casserole.

Caldeirada
(Portuguese Fish Stew)

The ingredients for this stew can contain almost any fish caught off our coast. Portuguese fishermen cook this dish for themselves on their long fishing trips around the Atlantic.

As a result there are no firm rules, only guidelines. It differs from the French Mediterranean bouillabaisse mainly in the choice of fish.

To serve 6 – 8

3 lb mix of fish (boned and skinned fillets of cod, coley, flounder, bass, hake or mullet – anything cheap on the day)

1 lb mussels (in the shell)

8 oz. frozen prawns (optional)

1 lb frozen squid, boned, cleaned and cut into rings

4 cloves garlic, peeled and roughly chopped

2 onions, finely sliced

4 tomatoes, peeled and chopped

2 lb potatoes, scrubbed and sliced

A handful, fresh coriander, roughly chopped

5 fl. oz. olive oil

1 pint. dry white wine

$1/2$ pint water

Salt & freshly ground black pepper

Method

Place each ingredient in a large casserole or stewpot, add seasoning and drizzle some oil and wine on each layer as you go. Start with half the sliced onion and follow with the potato and garlic, then half the tomatoes, followed by the fish, squid and prawns, the coriander, then the rest of the tomato and finally, the remaining onion slices. Pour over the remaining oil, water and wine, cover and bring to the boil. Turn down the heat and stew gently on top of the oven or in a slow oven for 30 or 40 minutes, until the potato is cooked. Meanwhile, wash and clean the mussels, ensuring all are alive, and place them on top of the stew when it is about to be served. When they open, the stew is cooked. Serve in deep bowls with thick slices of homemade bread.

Menu for a celebratory dinner for 8 people

Fricasse of rabbets and chicken
A leg of mutton boiled
Three carp in a dish
A great dish of a side of lamb
A dish of roasted pigeons
A dish of four lobsters
Three tarts
A lamprey pie, a most rare pie
A dish of anchovie
Good wine of many sorts

Samuel Pepys, 1663

CHAPTER THREE

GAME BIRDS & OTHER FOWL

I find chicken quite the most boring of meats but there are recipes that make the most of it – not a lot – but a few! I have chosen those I find tolerable. Most game birds are best served roasted, but by the end of the shooting season we tend to prefer pheasant cooked in a sauce and, as a result, I have included one or two ideas for late season suppers.

Spiced Wings

This is the perfect 'Fat boy' snack. They can be eaten any time of the day. Excellent as a starter at a summer barbecue or warm in front of a blazing fire and your favourite television programme. They were made famous in the States as 'The Anchor Bar Buffalo Wings' and the sauce that went with them is available on the internet. I think it is fun to design your own sauce however, although I give below one I think goes well with the wings.

To serve 4

16 fresh whole chicken wings

For the sauce

4 oz. brown sugar

Juice from 2 lemons

1 tbsp. finely grated fresh ginger

2 tbsp. tomato puree (optional)

4 tbsp. soy sauce

1 tsp. English mustard powder

1 tsp. salt

$1/2$ tsp. black pepper

6 fl. oz. water

1 tbsp. cornstarch

Method

Remove the tips from the chicken wings and either discard them or freeze them for use in making chicken stock at a later time. With a sharp knife, cut each wing in half through the joint and wash them in running water. Dry the wings on kitchen paper and place them in a single layer in an oven-proof pan. Bake in a hot oven for around 30 minutes, turning once. While the chicken is baking, mix together the sugar, cornstarch, salt and pepper in a saucepan, add the water, lemon juice and soy sauce and simmer, stirring constantly, until the sauce thickens. Brush the sauce onto the wings and continue baking, basting from time to time with the sauce, for a further 30 minutes until the wings are well cooked. Serve hot with lots of paper towels to take care of sticky fingers. We don't want the beer glass slipping through our fingers!

Chicken Belgrano

Don't ask me why this is named after General Belgrano. It does, however, originate in Argentina and is an excellent alternative to the usual bland dishes commonly served as Chicken Maryland, or worse, Coronation Chicken! The vegetable mixture should be piquant and highly seasoned.

To serve 4 – 6

1 medium sized chicken with its liver

1/2 lb sliced chorizo sausage

2 large onions, sliced

2 green peppers, deseeded and sliced

1/2 pint each white wine vinegar and water

Juice of 2 lemons

6 cloves garlic, finely chopped

1 chilli pepper, finely chopped

2 tbsp. fresh oregano, chopped (less if using dried)

4 eggs

Butter and breadcrumbs for garnish

Salt & freshly ground black pepper

Method

Marinade the chicken in a mix of the water, vinegar, half the lemon juice, one sliced onion and half the garlic in a large casserole for at least 3 hours. Place the casserole, covered, in a hot oven and cook for 1 or 2 hours until the chicken is well cooked and can be boned easily. Slice the meat and set aside. In butter, fry the remaining sliced onion, chorizo sausage, green peppers, chopped chicken liver, remaining garlic, oregano and chilli pepper. Season well with plenty of salt and pepper, add the remaining lemon juice and allow to cool. The mixture should be dry, sharp and spicy. Beat the eggs and blend into the chorizo mixture. Place a layer of sliced chicken in the bottom of a casserole dish and cover with some of the egg mixture, another layer of chicken on top and so on until all the mixture and chicken is used up. Put dabs of butter on top and sprinkle with the breadcrumbs. Cook in a hot oven for 15 minutes or so, until set and cooked through. Serve in the casserole in which it was cooked.

Confit of Duck

Confit of duck sounds grand but it is simply duck legs cooked and preserved in fat. The resultant meat is both tender and extremely succulent. It can be prepared well in advance and stored in a container until required. It is best served as an accompaniment to roast duck breast.

To serve 4

4 duck legs, whole with their skin

2 lb duck fat (can be bought in jars in most delicatessens)

1 oz. sea salt

1 tsp. ground black pepper

Pinch of nutmeg

Method

Rub the duck legs with the salt, place in a container with the pepper and a pinch of nutmeg, and leave in the refrigerator for 12 hours or so. When ready to cook, remove from the fridge and wipe off surplus salt. Fry the legs in a large heavy-based pan for 30 minutes or so until the fat begins to run and they turn slightly brown. Cover with sufficient fat and continue to cook in a hot oven for 2 hours or until the duck is very tender. Remove from the heat, place the legs in a jar or deep-sided container and cover completely with fat. When cool, store in the fridge for a week or more until required. To serve, heat the container gently to melt the fat, remove the legs and fry them on high heat until the skin crisps. Best served with roast duck breast, pickled cabbage and fried potatoes.

Game Pie

This traditional English pie can be made with a mix of partridge, pheasant, grouse, chicken or duck. The most important thing is to ensure there is plenty of flavour in the jelly. This is a great standby for those drop-in's around Christmas and New Year. It requires a lot of preparation but is simple to cook.

Pastry

1 lb plain flour

2 egg yolks

8 oz. butter

5 fl. oz. ice cold water

Salt

Filling

1 chicken or 2 or 3 game birds

8 oz. cooked ham

8 oz. lean pork

1 flat tsp. each of powdered mace, nutmeg and allspice

Salt & pepper

Forcemeat

4 oz. smoked bacon or smoked ham

12 oz. lean pork

8 oz. back pork fat

2 eggs

1 tbsp. chopped parsley

$1/2$ tsp. each dried basil and marjoram

$1/2$ tsp. each nutmeg and cayenne pepper

Salt & pepper

Stock

Pork skin and bacon rinds

Chicken and game bird bones

1 each carrot, onion and celery stick, sliced

1 tbsp. vinegar, (gelatine if needed)

Bouquet garni

Gelatine if needed

Salt & pepper

Method

To make the pastry, sift the flour and salt into a bowl, rub in the butter and then the egg yolks and a little water and work into a pliable paste. Split into two discs, one using $2/3$ for the base and the other $1/2$ for the top. Place both discs in the fridge, wrapped in clingfilm and rest for an hour or so. To prepare the filling, cut the pork and ham into $1/2$ inch cubes. Bone the chicken or game, remove the skin and cut the flesh into strips and season with the spices. For the forcemeat, mince the pork, bacon and pork fat in a food processor and blend in the beaten eggs, herbs and spices. To prepare the stock, boil the bones from the carcasses with the pork skin and bacon rinds, the vegetables, herbs and vinegar and salt and pepper. Simmer for at least 3 hours, then strain and reduce until the flavour is very concentrated. Check the seasoning. Test a little for setting and if necessary, add a little gelatine soaked in cold water. It is important that the stock be firm and flavourful. When all parts are prepared, assemble the pie by buttering a 9 inch pie mould and roll the pieces of pastry until they are about $1/4$ inch thick. Fit the larger piece into the mould leaving a 1 inch overhang. Line the pastry with a thin layer of forcemeat and put in the meat filling. Pack the remainder of the forcemeat around the meat and cover with the pastry lid, sealing the edges with water. Decorate the top of the pie with any remaining pastry and make a small hole at the top of the pie for escaping steam. Bake in a hot oven for about 30 minutes until the pastry is set and turning brown. Reduce the heat and cook, covered by foil, for a further 2 hours. Remove from the oven and add the stock through the hole at the top of the pie using a small funnel. This is sometimes a slow process, as the stock needs to settle around the meat. Allow to cool in the larder and keep for a few days to allow the flavour to develop.

Somerset Style Pheasant in Cream and Apple Brandy

Towards the end of the shooting season we like to eat the pheasant we have lying in the freezer, in this manner. Sometimes the birds may have been badly shot or suffered a bit on retrieval and cooking them in this way disguises the problems. Apart from anything else, the richness of the sauce makes a simple and most delicious meal.

To serve 4

A brace of pheasant, plucked, cleaned and oven ready

5 oz. butter

1 pint double cream

4 eating apples, peeled, cored and sliced

1/4 pint English apple brandy

1 small onion, finely chopped

1 tsp. brown sugar

1 clove garlic, finely sliced

Salt & pepper

Method

Melt the butter in a casserole dish and brown the birds on all sides. Cover and place the dish in a hot oven for 30 – 40 minutes until the birds are cooked. Allow to cool slightly then carve the breasts and legs into manageable pieces. Remove the skin and place the flesh in an oven-proof dish. Heat the cream and apple brandy and stir until it begins to thicken Season and pour over the pheasant. Serve with boiled rice. Fry the onion, garlic and apple rings in a little butter and the sugar until slightly caramelised and spread over the pheasant as a garnish.

Tony's Stuffed Chicken Breasts

I was quite determined not to include too many chicken dishes. They are usually so boring and anyway every cook knows chicken. These poached sausages, however, are an excellent stand-by for last-minute lunches or starters at supper parties. They are not that difficult to prepare and can be kept wrapped in clingfilm in the freezer or the fridge until required. The important thing is to ensure that the stuffing has plenty of flavour, which can be adjusted according to your personal taste and inclination.

To feed 4 as a light supper or as a starter for dinner

1 large chicken

1 large egg

2oz. tin anchovy fillets

1 tsp. grated nutmeg

1 onion, chopped

6 garlic cloves, chopped

1 $1/2$ tsp. curry powder (optional)

1 hot red chilli, chopped

Salt & freshly ground black pepper

Method

Cut off both sides of the chicken breast and remove the skin. Place each side in turn on a long piece of clingfilm, fold the clingfilm over the breast and hammer the meat until it is little more than an $1/4$ inch thick. Encourage it to form a square shape. Set aside, still wrapped in clingfilm. Remove the meat from the legs and thighs of the chicken, discard the skin, cut into pieces and place in a food processor with the chopped onion, anchovy, nutmeg, curry powder, garlic, chilli and egg. Blend to a paste and add plenty of seasoning. Gently peel back the top layer of clingfilm on each beaten breast and place half the stuffing across the centre. Carefully roll the meat into a sausage shape by folding the clingfilm around it. Be careful not to wrap the meat too tightly because it will expand somewhat when cooked. Ensure that the clingfilm at the ends of the sausage are twisted tight so that they remain closed whilst being cooked. Place the sausages in a pan of boiling water and simmer for at least 30 minutes. Check from time to time to ensure that the sausages are turned in the water so they are cooked through. Allow to cool and either store in the fridge until required, or remove the clingfilm and cut into $1/4$ inch slices. Serve on a piece of lettuce with a sweet and sour sauce (see page 134) or onion marmalade (see page 135).

Minted Chicken

This recipe was spotted in an Indian recipe book and adapted. You could add a couple of green chillies if you want to pepper it up a bit but, in any event, it is best enjoyed using very fresh mint from the garden.

To serve 4

8 chicken thighs, skinned and boned

2 large onions, sliced

2 garlic cloves, crushed

1 inch freshly grated ginger

3 tbsp. fresh mint, finely chopped

1 tsp. turmeric powder

3 tbsp. vegetable oil

2 green chillies, deseeded and chopped (optional)

Salt & pepper

Method

Fry the onions in the oil in a large flat-bottomed pot until they turn golden. Add the crushed garlic, ginger, turmeric and chillies (if used). Stir for a moment or two, add the chicken thighs and sauté for 15 minutes, turning the pieces over once. Carefully add a cup of water to the pot and continue cooking, uncovered, for a further 15 minutes or until the chicken is cooked. Add the mint, stir and continue cooking on medium heat for a further five minutes or so. Remove the chicken thighs and keep warm in a serving dish. Reduce the sauce and pour over the chicken and serve hot with couscous or rice.

Mawmenny
(Medieval English Spiced Poached Chicken Pudding)

I have adapted this ancient recipe, the origin of blancmange, as a cold light supper. It was introduced by the Crusaders in the 11th century and featured as part of banquets or feasts through the 12th and 13th centuries until finally the Victorians, who called it 'Shape', recreated it as a sweet pudding.

To serve 2 as a light supper

2 slices of white bread, crusts removed

2 chicken breasts, chopped

1 onion, chopped

2 tbsp. ground almond

1 tsp. ground cumin

$1/2$ tsp. ground cloves

1 tsp. ground ginger

1 egg

Salt & freshly ground black pepper

Method

Put the slices of bread in a blender and crumb. Add the chicken breasts and blend. Add the egg, ground almond, chopped onion and all the spices and continue to blend until the mixture turns into a thick paste. Pour the mixture into a suitable mould or small bowl and place in a larger pan or bain-marie of boiling water. Boil for 20 minutes then remove from the heat and allow to cool. When cool enough to handle, remove the bowl from the water, turn it upside down on a plate and shake the pudding out. Serve cold, cut into slices with tomato sauce or onion marmalade (see page 135).

Squire Hastings

I have found a description of a nobly-born squire of the old school, called Hastings from Devon, who is described in a book written in 1680 by Anthony Ashley Cooper, Earl of Shaftesbury. He might well have been describing any one of many Devon squires of the period in the following way:–

"...*he was low, very strong and very active with reddish flaxen hair, his clothes always green cloth and never all worth when new five pound... his house was perfectly of the old fashion... the great hall strewed with marrow bones, full of hawk's perches, hounds, spaniels and terriers, the upper sides of the hall hung with the foxes skins of this and last years killing, here and there a polecat intermixed; guns, keepers and huntsmen's poles in abundance... an oyster table at the lower end which was of constant use twice a day all the year round, for he never failed to eat oysters before dinner and supper through all seasons... the parlour was a long large room as poorly furnished; on a great hearth paved with brick lay some terriers and the choicest hounds and spaniels... on the side of the room was a door to an old chapel not used for devotion; the pulpit as the safest place, was not wanting of a cold chine of beef, pasty of venison, gammon of bacon or great apple pie with thick crust extremely baked... he drank a glass or two of wine at meals very often syrup of gilliflower in his sack and always a tun glass without feet stood by him holding a pint of small beer which he often stirred with a great sprig of rosemary... he was well natured but soon angry, calling his servants bastard and cuckoldry knaves, in one of which he often spoke truth to his knowledge and sometimes in both, though of the same man... he lived to a hundred and never lost his sight... and got to horse without help until past fourscore he rode to the death of a stag or fox as well as any!*"

He would, without doubt, have been a 'Fat boy' candidate.

CHAPTER FOUR

LAMB

As we live in Devon, we naturally believe there is no better lamb than the spring lambs born early in the year and fed on the rough and rugged slopes of Dartmoor. There is a sweetness to the meat that is not found elsewhere. It is even superior to the young Welsh or Scottish lambs sold, with much trumpeting, in all the supermarkets across the country. It also has a depth of flavour not found in the lambs produced in 10 weeks on farms in lowland Britain or the pale, tasteless rubbish sold in Europe. Because of this habit of getting meat to the shops as early as possible there is a risk that we will forget the taste of hog meat or mutton. Some dishes taste so much better using the meat of a mature animal cooked in a slow oven. I have included here dishes that benefit from being prepared with both lamb and mutton (if you can get it).

Moroccan Lamb Stew (Tagine)

A medieval recipe I have seen for a Persian variation of this Moroccan tagine recommends the meat be stewed without first frying. I prefer, however, to lightly fry the meat before adding water and the other ingredients.

To serve 4 – 6

A boned leg or shoulder of lamb, cut into chunks about 3/4 inch

For the spice paste:–

1 large onion, chopped

4 cloves garlic, finely chopped

1 tbsp. of grated fresh ginger,

1/2 tsp. grated nutmeg,

1 tsp. each sea salt, black pepper and paprika

3 tsp. each of whole cinnamon and coriander and cumin seeds

1/2 tsp. ground chilli powder

For the rest:–

12 dried apricots

Selection of other dried fruit such as sultanas, currants or preserved lemons

2 tbsp. olive oil

2 oz. butter

1 lb fresh spinach

2 oz. ground almonds

Sea salt and pepper

Method

Pound the whole spices in a pestle and mortar, together with the remaining spice ingredients, to form a paste. Mix the meat and spice paste in a bowl ensuring the meat is well coated with the mixture and leave in the fridge for an hour or more for the flavours to infuse. Clean the spinach and dunk in salted boiling water for a moment or two and refresh in cold water. Put the oil and butter in a large heavy pot and stir in the meat and spice mixture over a high heat until sealed and browned. Add the fruit, nuts and spinach with a glass or two of water, cover the pot and cook on low heat or in a low oven for about 2 – 3 hours until the meat is tender. Stir occasionally to avoid sticking and add a little stock if the stew becomes too dry. Adjust seasoning. The result should be a dry, sweet and spicy stew. Serve with couscous scattered with fresh mint in season.

Moroccan Lamb Pie

Prepare the meat and spinach as above and allow to cool. Butter a deep cake tin and lay a sheet of fila pastry on the bottom, allowing the ends to hang over the sides. Butter the sheet within the tin and add a further sheet at a different angle. Continue with several sheets buttering each layer allowing the pastry to hang out around the edge of the tin. Spoon in the cool lamb mixture and then cover with more overlapping, buttered sheets of fila to form a pie. Cook in a preheated oven at 200°c for about 30 minutes until the top is well browned. Carefully remove the pie from the cake tin and put it back in the oven for a further 30 minutes. Serve with yoghurt.

Roast Marinated Lamb

There are several marinades you can use to prepare this dish and to add flavour to the meat. The fun is designing one of your own. You could, for example, use ground cumin seeds instead of rosemary and lemon juice instead of orange, however, this is my choice.

To serve 4 – 6

Leg of lamb, boned

3 tbsp. runny honey

8 fl. oz. orange juice

3 cloves garlic, crushed

1 inch ginger, finely grated

2 tbsp. soy sauce

2 tbsp. red wine vinegar

1 tbsp. fresh rosemary, if available, otherwise 2 tsp. dried rosemary

Freshly ground pepper

Method

Marinade the meat the day before it is intended to be served. Place the joint in a dish or container just large enough to take it. Mix the orange juice, honey, soy sauce, garlic, rosemary and ginger and pour over the meat and leave in the fridge overnight or longer, turning the joint from time to time. When ready to cook, remove the joint from the marinade, put it in a hot oven in a small roasting tin. Roast for 25 – 30 minutes, then pour the marinade over the meat and continue to roast for a further 30 minutes, or a little less if a pink centre is desired. Remove any surplus fat from the juices, carve and serve with the gravy and roast vegetables and couscous instead of potatoes.

Pot Roast of Mutton

This is a traditional old English recipe with one or two embellishments. It may not be possible to find any mutton, so a cheap frozen shoulder of imported lamb will do nicely. No point wasting a shoulder of good new season West Country lamb for this slow-cooked dish.

To serve 4 or 6

1 shoulder of mutton or mature lamb, boned, rolled and tied

1 cinnamon stick

10 cloves

3 tbsp. brown sugar

2 preserved lemons, cut into 8 pieces

2 glasses port or Madeira

1 tsp. Chinese five spices powder (Wu Siang Fen)

Salt & pepper

Method

Mix all the ingredients together and rub onto the lamb in a casserole dish. Allow to stand, covered, in the fridge for a couple of days or until required, turning the meat from time to time. Remove from the fridge when you are ready to cook and allow the meat to stand for 30 minutes or so. Add sufficient water to reach halfway up the lamb and bring to a simmer on the stove. Cover with a lid and place in a slow oven for 3 – 4 hours, basting from time to time. When cooked and tender, remove from the casserole and place on a serving dish in a slow oven to keep warm. Pour the cooking liquor through a sieve and reduce on high heat. Skim off any surplus fat and reserve the liquid as gravy. The joint is best carved in thick slices and served with mashed potato and carrots.

Spiced Leg of Lamb
(West Indian Style)

This way of cooking an old, frozen leg of lamb is a favourite of ours in the winter and is simple to prepare.

To serve 4

4 – 5 lb leg of lamb, boned but not rolled

1 tbsp. salt

1 tbsp. ground black pepper

$1/2$ tbsp. cinnamon

2 tsp. nutmeg

2 tbsp. butter

1 medium onion, finely chopped

4 cloves garlic, finely chopped

5 oz. brown sugar

4 tbsp. malt vinegar

1 large wine glass of dark rum

Stuffing

$1/2$ lb Sausage meat and 3 slices bread, crumbed

1 tsp. each of ground cloves, ginger and allspice

1 egg

Salt & freshly ground black pepper

Method

Prick the joint all over with a fork. Blend together the salt, pepper, cinnamon and nutmeg and rub the mixture into the meat. Allow the joint to stand for at least an hour, but longer if possible. Make the stuffing by blending the sausage meat, breadcrumbs, spices and egg in a blender and put the mixture on the boned leg. Roll up and tie the meat securely.

Melt the butter in a baking dish and fry the chopped onions. When brown, add the garlic, brown sugar, vinegar and rum and stir. Place the lamb in a baking dish, baste well with some of the sauce and cook in a moderate oven for 1 $1/2$ hours, basting often to glaze the meat. Add more sauce as required and when the meat is cooked, remove from the pan and allow it to stand, covered, for at least 10 minutes. Reduce any remaining sauce and serve with the meat, mixed roast vegetables and couscous.

Braised Leg of Mutton with Garlic and Beans

Cooking a leg of mutton with loads of garlic by braising it in a slow oven for 4 hours produces meat that can be eaten with a fork, with all the flavour retained.

To serve 4 – 6

1 leg of mutton or mature hill bred lamb

1 lb haricot beans

2 carrots, diced

2 onions, chopped

20 cloves garlic

1 bottle cheap red wine

14 oz. tin chopped tomatoes

2 oz. tin anchovy fillets

Bouquet garni to include rosemary, thyme and bay

Oil and butter for cooking

1 pint beef stock

Salt and black pepper

Method

Soak the beans overnight and in the morning, drain and cover with fresh water. Bring them to the boil and simmer for an hour or so with a dash of salt. Before they are fully cooked, remove from the heat and drain them.

Put some butter and oil in a pan and fry the onions until they start to brown then add the carrots, stirring all the time to avoid sticking. When they appear to be softening, remove the pan from the heat and reserve.

Place the leg of mutton in a buttered oven dish with the anchovy fillets and brown it on all sides. Add the vegetable mixture, garlic, bouquet garni, beans, stock and enough of the wine to ensure that the vegetables are covered. Season well, cover the dish and cook in the oven slowly for at least 4 hours, basting the meat from time to time and turning the joint every 30 minutes or so. The longer the meat is cooked the better. The dish is best cooked the day before and allowed to cool so that the fat can be skimmed off. Reheat and serve, carved thickly, with mashed potatoes and the beans that surrounded the joint.

Lamb Potjie

Potjie, a mild spicy stew from South Africa (pronounced poy-kee) was probably adapted from an old Cape Malay dish called denningvleis.

To serve 4 – 6

2 lbs lamb, cut into 1 inch chunks

2 large onions, sliced

5 or 6 garlic cloves

1 tbsp. crushed chillies

1 tsp. cumin seeds

1 tsp. garam masala

4 cardamom pods

1 tsp. fennel seeds

1 inch cinnamon stick

1 tsp. coriander seeds

1 cup of water

1 cup dried peaches

1 tbsp. sugar

Oil or butter for frying

Salt and pepper

A selection of seasonal vegetables, sliced

Method

Fry the onions together with the garlic and the crushed chillies until golden in a deep oven-proof pot. Add the meat and all the spices crushed, but not powdered and stir-fry until browned. Add the water, together with the peaches, sugar and salt and cook, covered, on low heat for 3 hours, until the meat is almost cooked. Add the vegetables in layers, season and continue to cook at a slow simmer until the meat is cooked through. Serve with boiled rice and sweet chutney.

Kibbeh
(Minced Stuffed Lamb Balls)

This recipe from the Lebanon takes a bit of time to prepare but is easy to cook. You can experiment with the ingredients for the stuffing, but I have given a basic one popular throughout the Middle East, the ingredients for which are easily obtained in most supermarkets or delicatessens. In all parts of the Middle East, the preparation of these little dumplings is thought to be the standard by which women of the household are judged. Guests would be able to judge the refinement and skill of the wife by the quality of the kibbeh she served even if it was her cook who made them.

To serve 4 (3 kibbehs each)
For the stuffing

6 oz. lean lamb, minced

1 small onion, finely chopped

1 level tsp. each, ground allspice & cinnamon

2 oz. pine nuts, lightly toasted

1 handful coriander, roughly chopped

Olive oil

$1/2$ glass water

Sea salt & freshly ground black pepper

For the casing

9 oz. lean lamb, finely minced

5 oz. fine bulgur wheat, washed

$1/2$ small onion, grated

Sea salt & freshly ground black pepper

Method

To make the stuffing, fry the onion until well browned, add the lamb, spices and stir, ensuring the lamb is well broken up. Add a little water, season with salt and pepper and simmer until the water has evaporated. Place the meat in a bowl and stir in the pine nuts and coriander. Leave to cool slightly.

To make the casing, grind the well seasoned meat and the onion in a food processor with a little water to form a paste. Wash the bulgur wheat and blend into the meat mixture.

To form the kibbeh, wet your hands and take enough of the casing mixture to form a ball the size of a golf ball. Flatten the ball into an oval shape, make a hole in one end with a finger in order to hollow out the kibbeh, ensuring that the sides are as thin as possible. Fill the hollow with a teaspoon or so of the stuffing mixture and gently seal the opening, ensuring that the oval shape is re-formed. Continue with the rest of the mixture – you should have enough for twelve egg-shaped ovals. When you have used all the mixture and are ready to eat, fry the kibbeh in hot olive oil until well browned and firm to the touch. Serve with minted yoghurt and a green salad.

Bobotie

This simple minced lamb dish is popular in the Cape district of South Africa and like Potjie is very easy to make.

To serve 4 – 6

2 lbs minced lamb

2 slices of white bread, trimmed

2 cups milk to soak

1 medium sized onion finely chopped

4 cloves garlic, crushed

1 tsp. crushed fresh ginger

2 tbsp. curry powder

1 tsp. ground turmeric

Butter for frying

2 eggs

Juice of 1 lemon

$1/2$ cup raisins or sultanas

$1/2$ cup slivered almonds

$1/2$ cup chutney or apricot jam

4 bay leaves

Salt & pepper

Method

Soak the bread in half the milk, squeeze out excess liquid and retain milk. Crumble bread into the minced meat. Fry the onions in most of the butter until golden. Add the curry powder, ginger, garlic, lemon juice and turmeric, stir constantly for about a minute and set aside in a dish to keep warm. Put the meat and bread mixture into the pan with the remaining butter and cook for about five minutes until the meat changes colour. Remove from the heat and add the fried onion mixture, one egg lightly beaten, half the milk, the raisins, slivered almonds and chutney and mix well in a mixing bowl.

Pour the mixture into a greased oven dish. Beat together the remaining milk and egg, season and pour over the mixture. Press the bay leaves lightly into the top and bake for 30 minutes in a preheated oven at 180°c until golden brown. Serve with boiled yellow rice, sweet chutney and a green salad.

Lancashire Hotpot

I remember eating hotpot when I was a boy, soon after the War, when meat was rationed and it was a real treat to eat mutton let alone lamb. A hotpot is always served in the lidless dish in which it is cooked. Unlike so many stews, the meat is boiled without first being browned and a true hotpot will always contain oysters – a hangover, I suspect, from the days when oysters were the poor mans food. The secret is, of course, to cook it slowly. In Liverpool the dish is known as 'scouse', where it might contain chopped carrots and barley.

To serve 4 – 6

2 lb scrag end of mutton or lamb chops

2 onions, thinly sliced

2 sheep kidneys, cut into quarters

1 dozen oysters, shucked (optional)

5 oz. button mushrooms (optional)

1/2 pint beef stock

2 lb potatoes, peeled and thickly sliced

1/2 oz. butter

Salt & pepper

Method

Brush some of the butter around the inside of a deep pot and place a layer of potatoes in the bottom. Remove as much fat as possible and any bone chippings from the chops and arrange them on the potatoes. Scatter the kidney quarters, mushrooms and oysters (if used) evenly around the meat and season well. Add the sliced onions and the rest of the potatoes, ensuring that the top layer is neatly arranged. Pour in the stock and brush the top layer of potato with the remaining butter. Cover with a piece of greaseproof paper and cook in a slow oven for at least 4 hours. Half an hour before the dish is ready, remove the greaseproof paper, check the level of liquid adding more stock if required and return to the oven for 10 minutes to brown.

Stuffed Breast of Lamb

Breast of lamb is the cheapest cut you can buy but, if treated properly, it makes a most delicious meal. Every Middle Eastern country has its own way of preparing this dish but here I have chosen to include an Armenian version that combines dried fruit, cracked wheat and spinach in an irresistible combination.

To serve 2 greedy ones

1 breast lamb

1 large onion, finely chopped

10 oz. frozen leaf spinach

4 oz. cracked wheat

3 oz. pine nuts

2 oz. seedless raisins

2 oz. dried apricots

1 egg, beaten

1 handful chopped parsley

1 handful chopped mint

1/4 pint white wine

Salt & freshly ground black pepper

Butter for cooking

Method

Bone the breast, carefully removing all gristle and trim off as much excess fat as possible. Season well with salt and black pepper on both sides. Defrost the spinach, squeeze out as much liquid as possible, chop finely and place in a bowl. Fry the onion in butter until golden and add to the bowl together with all other ingredients except the wine, season and mix well. Allow the mixture to stand for half an hour or so to allow the remaining liquid to be absorbed by the cracked wheat. Spread the stuffing thinly over the underside of the lamb and roll up from the thin end. Should there be any stuffing left over place in a small overnproof dish and cook in a slow oven to serve with the meat. Tie with string and place in a casserole as close to the size of the meat as possible. Pour in the wine, cover and place in a hot oven for around 25 minutes. Reduce the heat and cook for at least 3 hours. The juices in the casserole, once the fat is removed, can be reduced, seasoned and used as a thin gravy.

Serve with cabbage or sprouts.

Lamb Shank

This is another cheap cut of lamb which again produces a delicious meal. The sauce is rich and spicy and, if the meat is cooked slowly for at least five hours in a slow oven or the bottom of an Aga, it will fall off the bone. It is always better to cook this dish the day before and reheat it slowly when required.

To serve 4

4 lamb shanks

1 tsp. each coriander seeds, oregano and dried red chilli

1 tbsp. fresh rosemary, finely chopped

1 tbsp. rough sea salt

Flour for dusting

1 tbsp. olive oil

2 oz. butter

6 cloves garlic, chopped

2 onions, chopped

2 carrots, chopped

2 celery sticks, chopped

1 2 oz. tin anchovy fillets

1 14 oz. tin chopped tomato

8 fl. oz. red wine

3 tbsp. balsamic vinegar

Method

Mash the coriander seeds, oregano, chilli, rosemary, chopped garlic and salt in a pestle and mortar and rub the mixture into the lamb shanks. Allow to stand for a couple of hours. Dust lightly with flour and brown the shanks on all sides in the butter and oil in an ovenproof casserole. When well browned, remove the shanks from the dish and keep warm. Fry the onions, carrots and celery until soft, add the vinegar and stir for 2 or 3 minutes. Add the anchovies, red wine and the tomatoes, stirring all the time. The anchovy fillets will dissolve in the juice. Add the lamb shanks and bring to the boil. Put the lid on the casserole dish and place it in the bottom oven of the Aga, or any other oven at about 170°c, for at least 5 hours, turning the meat occasionally. When well cooked, remove from the oven and allow to cool slowly with the lid on. When cold, store the casserole in the fridge until required. When ready to serve, skim off the fat on the surface, remove the shanks and vegetables from the casserole and set aside. Pass the cooking juices through a colander and boil vigorously until they are reduced by half then lower the heat, return the shanks and vegetables to the sauce and heat through. Best served with the vegetables from the casserole and well-buttered mashed potatoes or celeriac. The sauce should be dark, thick and spicy.

To Dress Beife Stakes

"Take goode buttock Beife and cut it in thinn slices, chop it as you doe for Scotch Scollops wash them all over with Eggs on both sides and strew them over pretty thick with Crumbs of bred mixt with sweet herbs, a little pepper and salt, fry them with very little licquor for the sauce take a little Gravy, Anchovie, butter and Lemon if you plees…"

To Drawe Gravey

"Take sum slices of buttock Beife hack it with ye back of a knife put into a fry pan fry them with a little fresh butter just enuf to brown then put in a pint of water an onyon a bunch of sweet herbs a little whole pepper and 2 or 3 anchovies so let it stew lesurly over ye fire till half ye licquor is wasted then squeese out the juice of ye meat between 2 trenchers and keep it for your use…"

From a 17th Century Recipe Book

Dandelion

Dandelion leaves were used to flavour salads as early as the 11th century. The name comes from the Norman French, 'dent-de-lion', lions tooth, because of the shape of the leaf. They were also known as 'pissenlit' in France as a result of their supposed diuretic properties.

CHAPTER FIVE

BEEF

Long before roast beef became the fashion in English households, the most effective way to cook a joint of beef was in a 'baking oven'. This was a large cast iron pot with a close fitting lid which was placed in the ashes of the fire. In Devon, farmers depended on peat for fuel and peat was not suitable for roasting meat. The farmers' wives would load what was to be cooked into the baking oven and bury it in the fire, raking hot ashes to cover the pot. They would then leave the meat to cook slowly all day until it was produced for the evening meal. Families developed their own particular favourite recipes for cooking in this manner.

In the 1950's, I can remember accompanying an old school chum on an exeat to his mother's house for Sunday lunch. I will never forget the delicious sense of anticipation, waiting to dunk thick slices of home-made bread in the juices in the pan after the roast beef was moved to a carving platter by his mother's cook. Heaven! But then we had to sit and eat every last scrap of food on our plates before being allowed to leave the table.

Roast Beef

Roasting meat is not just a question of putting the joint in a pan and the pan in the oven and forgetting about it. The first step is to choose a well-marbled, open – grained piece of meat and check with your butcher that it has been well hung. If the meat is bright red with shiny white fat – reject it. To ensure the perfect roast, allow the meat to stand outside the fridge for an hour or two to reach room temperature before roasting. Do not salt beef before cooking, as the salt will draw out juices and never put sliced meat in the oven or under a grill to keep warm, it will dry out and turn grey.

To serve 4 – 8

A 7 lb sirloin or forerib of well hung English beef on the bone (at least 4 ribs)

Butter or dripping,

Freshly ground black pepper

For the Yorkshire puddings

4 oz. plain flour

$1/2$ level tsp. salt

1 large egg

$1/4$ pint milk

$1/4$ pint water

Dripping or butter

Method

Prick the surface of the meat and season well with freshly ground black pepper. Place the joint on a grid in a hot roasting tin in the hot oven of the Aga. Allow 15 minutes to the pound plus 15 minutes for a rare joint, a further 15 minutes for a medium rare joint and longer for a well-done joint. Baste every 15 – 20 minutes. Should you be cooking the joint in an electric or gas oven, start cooking at about 230°c and after about 20 minutes, reduce the temperature to 200°c. Add peeled, parboiled potatoes, 3 or 4 onions and any other roasting vegetables to the juices surrounding the joint an hour or so before the meat is cooked and ensure they are turned from time to time. Remove the joint from the oven, season well with salt and pepper and cover loosely with tinfoil. Allow it to stand for at least 15 minutes before carving. When the meat and vegetables have been removed, pour the fat gently from the tin, taking care to leave all the juices and bits of meat that remain. Add a little stock or red wine, salt and pepper and stir. Do not add flour – beef gravy should not be too thick.

Mix the batter for the Yorkshire puddings until it has the consistency of thick cream and allow it to stand for at least 20 minutes. Preheat a bun or Yorkshire pudding tray with $1/4$ inch of dripping or butter in each section. Fill the sections of the tray almost to the top with the batter and cook in a hot oven for 25 minutes until the puddings are brown and crisp. Don't open the door of the Aga or oven during cooking or the puddings won't rise.

Corned Beef Hash

There are as many different ways of preparing this dish as there are of preparing beef stew. This, my favourite, was picked up in Canada.

To serve 4
1 lb tin corned beef, cut into cubes

1 lb potatoes, peeled and diced

2 shallots, finely chopped

$1/2$ pint of milk

4 pickled walnuts

4 pieces of toast

Dripping or butter for frying

Worcestershire sauce

Salt & pepper

Method
Melt the dripping or butter in a pan and sauté the potatoes, add the chopped shallots and season. When the shallots have softened but before they turn brown, add the corned beef.

Continue cooking, stirring occasionally. Bring the milk to the boil and add a little at a time. The potatoes will absorb the milk as they cook. Add a splash or two of Worcestershire sauce. When the potato is cooked and soft remove the pan from the heat and spoon a portion of the mixture onto each piece of toast. Place them under the grill to brown. Serve on individual plates with a pickled walnut on top of each helping.

Beef Cecils

Although tradition dictates that these are made with leftover roast beef, in fact, minced or chopped meat of any kind has been used in the past to make this 18th century dish, made famous by a Cecil family chef.

To serve 4 – 6
4 slices roast beef, minced or very finely chopped

$1/2$ pint white breadcrumbs

1 onion, finely chopped

3 anchovy fillets, chopped

$1/2$ tsp. grated lemon peel

1 pinch ground nutmeg

2 tbsp. parsley, finely chopped

1 oz. melted butter

1 egg, beaten

Flour

Salt & pepper

Method
Blend together the minced beef and all other ingredients except the flour and egg. Season and form the mixture into balls the size of duck eggs. Roll these in some flour, dip them in the beaten egg, roll in the breadcrumbs and fry them until brown all over. Serve with onion gravy and mashed potatoes.

To make the onion gravy
Finely slice 2 onions and fry in butter until they turn brown, add $1/2$ pint beef stock, a glass or two of red wine, season well and stir in a desert spoon of honey, serve hot with the Beef Cecils.

Cottage Pie

The original cottage pie was always made with leftover beef and shepherd's pie with minced, cooked lamb or mutton. They are both practical, tasty and easy ways of creating an extra dish from the remains of a Sunday joint. Below is a recipe for cottage pie, but a similar recipe could be used for making a shepherd's pie if you replace the tomato ketchup with a few anchovy fillets, which melt when fried, and go so well with the minced lamb or mutton.

To serve 4 or 5

1 lb minced or finely chopped, cooked beef

1 large onion, peeled and chopped

1 carrot, diced

1 parsnip, diced

1/4 pint beef or chicken stock

1 Oxo cube

1 tbsp. each tomato ketchup and concentrated tomato puree

1 tbsp. Worcestershire sauce

1 tbsp. mixed dried herbs

1 tbsp. butter

2 lb potatoes

Some butter and milk for the potatoes

Salt & freshly ground black pepper

Method

In a heavy pot, fry the onion in butter until golden, add the diced vegetables and stir-fry for a few minutes. Add the minced meat, continue to stir for a minute or two then pour in the stock and allow it to bubble up. Now crumble in the oxo cube, add the Worcestershire and tomato ketchup and concentrate and simmer uncovered on low heat to allow it to thicken. Check seasoning and pour the mixture into a suitable ovenproof dish to cool – this is important – hot mashed potato added at this stage would sink into the meat and gravy and spoil the appearance of the pie. Peel and boil the potatoes, drain and mash with a little butter and a drop or two of milk. Season with salt and pepper and leave to stand for a few minutes. Spoon the mashed potato evenly over the cool meat mixture and drag a fork across the top to make decorative lines. At this point, the dish can be stored in the fridge until required. To serve, dot with butter and place the dish under the grill or in a hot oven for 20 minutes until the top browns. Serve with boiled cabbage or carrots cooked in a little water and butter with plenty of salt and pepper.

Pot Roast of Beef

I think this is an ideal dish for a winter dinner party. It can be cooked slowly in advance and reheated later when required. Although a pot roast by definition, is usually cooked on a hob, cooking in a slow oven or the bottom oven of an Aga is an alternative.

To serve 4

2 tbsp. chopped pancetta

14 fl. oz. strong red wine,

2 lb chuck steak

3 oz. chopped onion

2 tbsp. extra-virgin olive oil

2 cloves garlic, mashed

2 oz chopped celery

Sea salt & freshly ground black pepper

Method

Fry the chopped pancetta and olive oil in a heavy-bottomed pan for about a minute or so, stirring all the time. Add the joint of meat and brown it on all sides. Remove the meat and set aside. Add the chopped onion and cook until it begins to turn golden. Return the meat to the pan together with the garlic, celery, salt and pepper and about 5 fl. oz. of the wine. Put the lid on the pan and simmer on very low heat for about 3 hours. Turn the meat from time to time adding the rest of the wine as the liquid reduces. If the cooking liquid evaporates before the meat is cooked, add a little stock or water in order to prevent the joint from sticking to the pan. The meat is cooked when it feels extremely tender when prodded with a fork. Take the meat out of the pan when it's cooked and let it rest for 15 minutes before slicing it very thinly. Arrange the slices on a serving dish, reheat the juices in the pan and pour over the meat. Serve immediately.

Hungarian Goulash

Goulash, a beef soup named after Magyar cowboys (gulyas), which has now developed into this spicy stew, dates back to the 9th century, before the foundation of the Hungarian state. There are many variants but I have chosen a simple and traditional recipe. There is some debate, even among Hungarians, as to what should and should not be included in the ultimate goulash. It is not even clear what this stew should be called. Some say goulash is a soup and the stew should be known as porkolt. Others insist it can be both a soup and a stew, but all agree it should be made with Hungarian paprika which is, of course, hard to find. I have chosen to base this recipe on one I found produced by a Hungarian chef in a New York restaurant. The typical case of 'this is how my mother made it back home in Budapest'. OK! Fine, we believe you! He placed emphasis on the fact that no tomato, tomato concentrate or tomato sauce should ever be included in a true Hungarian goulash – why? God knows! Purists also agree the stew should not contain flour, soured cream or wine – but you decide.

To serve 6 or 4 hungry ones

2 lb beef shin

1 $1/2$ tbsp. sweet Hungarian paprika (Spanish will do fine)

1 tbsp. hot paprika or cayenne pepper

2 onions, finely chopped

10 cloves of garlic, finely chopped

1 lb potatoes, peeled and diced

1 pint beef stock

Buttered noodles (spaetzle, according to the Hungarian chef)

2 oz. lard

Salt & freshly ground black pepper

Method

Cut the beef into 2 inch chunks. Combine the paprikas and roll the beef chunks in a half of it. Melt half the lard in a large casserole and brown the beef on all sides. Remove the meat, roll it in the remaining paprika and keep it warm on the stove. Fry the chopped onions and garlic in the remaining lard in the same casserole until they become soft. Scrape the bottom of the casserole to include any bits of meat and paprika that stick to the bottom, replace the meat, add the stock and diced potatoes. Ensure the meat is covered by the stock or add water if required. Bring to the boil and then place in a slow oven to simmer for 2 hours or longer until the meat is tender and the potatoes are cooked and melting into the sauce. Check the seasoning and allow to cool. Place the casserole in the fridge overnight to allow the fat to set on the top. Remove the fat with a slotted spoon before reheating. I am told this fat is wonderful spread on a chicken before roasting. The resultant stew should be reddish in colour, rich and fiery. Serve on buttered noodles.

Moussaka

Moussaka from the Arabic muhklabah is the name in Greece for a layered pie made with minced beef and mixed vegetables topped with a white sauce. It is one of the dishes most identified with Greek food and is served as a family Sunday lunch, often cooked in the village baker's oven during mass. We tend to use minced beef, aubergine and potatoes but in Greece, I am told, they also use a mix of courgettes, tomatoes, pumpkin and peppers.

To serve 6

For the sauce

2 oz. butter (clarified if possible)

1 $1/2$ oz flour

2 egg yolks, beaten (optional)

1 pint milk

2 oz. grated Parmesan

$1/2$ tsp. grated nutmeg

Salt & pepper

For the rest

1 lb minced beef

2 onions, finely chopped

3 large aubergine

1 lb potatoes, peeled and thickly sliced

4 cloves garlic, finely chopped

$1/2$ tsp. sage

2 bay leaves

2 tbsp. concentrated tomato puree

Olive oil for frying

Salt & pepper

Method

Slice the aubergine $1/4$ inch thick and lay on a tray, sprinkle with salt and leave to sweat for 10 minutes or so. Rinse, pat dry and then fry them in oil until they turn light brown. Remove from the pan and rest on kitchen paper to drain. Fry the onions in a little oil, until they become soft, add the garlic and mince, fry until it is no longer pink, stir in the tomato concentrate, sage and bay leaves and set aside. Fry the potato slices in a little oil until they begin to colour but are not cooked through and set aside. To make the sauce, melt the butter in a small pan, and stir in the flour. Gradually add the milk stirring all the time over gentle heat, until it thickens. Bring to the boil and simmer for 5 minutes. Stir in the nutmeg and carefully beat in the egg yolks (if used). Fold in half the grated cheese and check the seasoning.

To assemble the moussaka, lay half the mince meat mixture on the bottom of an ovenproof dish. Place a layer of aubergine over it and some of the sauce, then more meat followed by a layer of potato. Repeat if more remains. Pour the balance of the sauce over the top so it completely covers the surface and sprinkle with the remaining grated cheese. Place the dish in a medium hot oven for 20 or 30 minutes or until cooked through and the top is golden. Serve hot with a simple green salad.

Boiled Brisket in Sauce

This is a great summer standby dish which is best served warm. Boiled brisket is easy to cook and delicious to eat. Yet again it is open to interpretation and there are many ways of varying the ingredients, depending on your pocket and what is available in the larder. We adapted this recipe from one we found in a newspaper and it has become a firm favourite.

To serve 6 – 8

3 lb rolled unsalted brisket of beef or similar joint

2 carrots roughly chopped

2 celery stalks halved

2 hard-boiled eggs

A handful of chopped parsley

1 onion, peeled and studded with cloves

1 tbsp. capers

2 tbsp. chopped gherkins

3 or 4 anchovy fillets

1 shallot, finely chopped

2 tbsp. breadcrumbs

2 tbsp. red wine vinegar

6 tbsp. good olive oil

Sea salt & freshly ground black pepper

Method

Place the meat and chopped vegetables in a saucepan of water and bring to the boil. Skim off any scum that comes to the surface. Simmer gently for at least 4 hours until the meat is tender. Leave the meat to cool in the liquid and prepare the sauce by pounding the anchovies, capers, egg yolks and a good pinch of sea salt in a mortar. Add the breadcrumbs, parsley and vinegar and check the seasoning before adding the oil. Roughly chop the egg whites and gherkins and mix into the sauce. Remove excess fat from the brisket and chop the meat into $1/2$ inch cubes or thick slices, mix with the sauce and serve warm.

Boiled Beef & Carrots

This is a solid favourite with all 'Fat boy' foodies. You can't beat this winter feast of boiled salt beef, carrots and dumplings to wrap around your ribs when the wind is blowing and the frost sets in.

To serve 6

For the dumplings

8 oz. plain flour

1 tsp. salt

1 tsp. baking powder

4 oz. suet, shredded and chopped

Water

For the meat

3 lb salt brisket, boned and rolled

1 tbsp. brown sugar

10 peppercorns

1 large parsnip, peeled and chopped into large pieces

1 lb carrots, peeled and sliced thickly

1 lb onions, peeled and quartered

1 large turnip, peeled and cut into chunks

Method

Soak the salt beef in water overnight. Dry and rub the lean meat with the sugar and let it stand for 30 minutes. Put it in a pan with the peppercorns and cover with cold water. Bring slowly to the boil, then cover and leave the meat to simmer for 2 hours.

After about an hour add the vegetables and continue simmering for at least another hour. Now start making the dumplings by mixing the flour, salt and baking powder and then knead in the suet. Gently trickle in the water until you have a soft dough. Form the dough into 8 or 10 small balls, roll them in flour and add them to the liquid when there is 15 minutes of cooking time left. Lift the meat out of the liquid and place it on a serving dish surrounded by the vegetables. The meat is also excellent cold. If you choose to serve it cold, let it stand in the liquid to keep moist until required.

Steak, Kidney and Oyster Pudding

Boiled puddings made with beef suet are among the oldest traditional English dishes and remain one of the most popular winter meals to this day. Boiling and roasting are traditionally the forms of cooking most understood in English houses. Pudding, derived from the Norman French, boudin, was originally a type of sausage. From the 16th century, dried peas or beans were tied up in a cloth suspended in the liquid of a stew, left cooking slowly in a pot over the open fire and eaten as the evening meal. I believe this dish may be the ultimate 'Fat boy' meal.

To serve 4 – 6

2 lb braising steak. chopped into $^1/_2$ inch cubes

8 oz. ox kidney, cored, skinned and chopped into $^1/2$ inch pieces

4 oz. field mushrooms, chopped into $^1/_2$ inch pieces

12 freshly shucked oysters

1 tbsp. vinegar

1 tbsp. plain flour

1 tbsp. finely chopped herbs (bay, parsley, thyme and sage)

1 onion, finely chopped

1 tbsp. Worcestershire sauce

1 glass port

Salt & pepper & paprika

For the suet crust

12 oz. self-raising flour

8 oz. best beef suet, well shredded

1 tsp. salt

8 fl. oz. ice cold water

Method

Sift the self-raising flour into a bowl with the salt and stir in the well shredded suet. Add cold water slowly to make a smooth paste that leaves the side of the bowl clean. Cut off one third of the pastry and roll into a circle for the lid. Roll out the rest of the dough until you have a big enough circle to line the bowl in which you intend to cook the pudding. Grease the bowl and line it with the dough, trimming the surplus from the top. Sprinkle the Worcestershire sauce over the meat and then toss it in the plain flour, paprika, salt and pepper. Scatter the oysters among the meat and mix with the mushrooms, chopped onion and herbs and pack loosely into the lined bowl. Pour over the glass of port, damp the edges of the pastry and seal the pudding with the lid, leaving a small hole in the centre to allow the steam to escape. Cover with tinfoil or a securely tied cloth and place the bowl in a steamer or large pot and fill to halfway up the bowl with boiling water. The water must be boiling. Boil or steam for 3 or 4 hours, topping up with boiling water when required. Remove the tinfoil or cloth, run a knife around between the pie and the bowl, place a deep plate on top of the bowl and invert. Remove the bowl and serve with mashed potatoes and boiled carrots with a generous dollop of butter on each.

Braised Oxtail

A great family favourite of ours, especially in the winter. Keep the meal simple. Don't be tempted to jazz it up – just stick to the oxtail, carrots, onions and boiled potatoes. Great 'Fat boy' food for a cold day.

To serve 4 – 6

3 lb oxtail, cut into joints by the butcher

3 pints beef stock

2 tbsp. dripping or butter

4 rashers streaky bacon, cubed

2 onions, roughly sliced

2 carrots, roughly sliced

2 parsnips, peeled and roughly chopped

1 stick of celery, chopped

Handful of flour

Bouquet garni: bay leaf, thyme, peppercorns and parsley stalks

Salt & black pepper

Method

Heat the dripping or butter in a large stewpan, put in the pieces of tail and brown well all over. Remove the meat and roll in a handful of seasoned flour and set aside. Put in the chopped vegetables and stir them around the pan about for a minute or two. Replace the meat, add the bouquet garni and stock, season well and bring to the boil. Place a lid tightly on the pan and simmer in a slow oven for 5 hours until the meat is about to fall off the bones. The dish is best left to stand overnight. To serve, remove the fat from the top with a slotted spoon, reheat, then remove the pieces of ox tail and pile in the centre of a serving dish and keep warm. Strain the gravy, bring to the boil and reduce. Adjust seasoning. If the gravy is a bit thin, add a teaspoon of cornflour and an oxo cube. The resultant gravy should be thick, dark and rich. Pour over the meat and serve with boiled potatoes, carrots and cabbage.

Exeter Stew with Herb Dumplings

It pays to make this stew with good quality meat and it is best done with sirloin or rump steak rather than stewing steak. The original recipe was found in a West Country cook book, where it was suggested that the stew could be left from early morning until late evening to cook in the hot ashes of an open fire, so we cook it in the bottom oven of an Aga.

To serve 4
For the dumplings

3 oz. plain flour

3 oz. beef suet, finely shredded and chopped

1/4 tsp. baking powder

2 tsp. finely chopped parsley

1/2 tsp. marjoram or savoury

Salt

Water

For the stew

1 1/2 lbs sirloin or rump steak

2 onions, chopped

2 each carrots, celery stalks and small white turnips, peeled and sliced

1 pint beef stock

1/2 pint rough farm cider, if available or add another 1/2 pint of beef stock

1 oz. butter

2 bay leaves

2 sprigs of rosemary, thyme and parsley, tied together

1/2 oz. plain flour seasoned with salt & freshly ground black pepper

Method

Cut the steak into 3/4 inch cubes and roll in the seasoned flour. Sauté the meat in the butter to brown on all sides, remove and set aside. Add the chopped onions to the pan and cook for 10 minutes or until the onions are golden. Return the meat to the pan and gradually add the stock, together with the herbs and cider, stirring constantly with a wooden spoon. Scrape the bottom of the pan to include any bits of meat or onion sticking there. Bring to the simmer and leave in a low oven for 4 hours or more. Add the chopped vegetables and continue to simmer for at least 1/2 hour. Whilst the stew is cooking, make the dumplings by blending the flour, baking powder and a little salt with the suet, working it in with your fingertips. Add the marjoram and parsley and a trickle of water, enough to make a smooth dough and form it into 8 small balls. Add the dumplings to the stew and continue to simmer for a further 1/2 hour. Check the seasoning and serve the meat and vegetables in a serving dish with the dumplings on top.

Chilli and Beans

I have always claimed that chilli con carne is arguably the best dish to come out of America. It has little, if anything to do with Mexico but is very popular in Texas and we love it well spiced.

To serve 4

1 large onion, chopped

6 cloves garlic, finely chopped

Oil for frying (any will do, but olive is best)

1 lb minced beef (not fillet steak)

1 tin chopped tomatoes

1 tin red kidney beans

2 glasses red wine

1 tbsp. tomato puree

Salt and black pepper

1/4 bar of rich dark chocolate

Spices

1/2 tbsp. dried oregano

1/2 tbsp. dried cumin

1/2 tbsp. paprika

1/2 tbsp. chilli powder

1 beef stock cube

2 bay leaves

Splash of Worcestershire sauce

Method

Fry the onions and garlic in the oil in a deep casserole until well browned and then stir in the spices, including the crumbled stock cube and cook for a moment or two. Add the mince and stir well to ensure it is browned all over. Add the chopped tomatoes, beans, red wine, tomato puree and salt and pepper and bring to a bubble. Place the casserole in a slow oven for 2 or 3 hours until the meat is tender, add the chocolate and stir until melted. Leave the casserole with the lid on to cool. This dish improves by being reheated and is best served with boiled long-grain rice.

Baked Stuffed Marrow

In September when marrows are cheap and plentiful they make an excellent supper dish and it's a doddle to make. Marianne tends to make more mince than is required for this dish alone and saves what's left over for another meal.

To serve 4

1 medium or large marrow

1 lb minced beef

2 onions, finely chopped

1 stick celery, finely chopped

2 carrots, finely chopped

4 cloves garlic, finely chopped

1 tbsp. Worcestershire sauce

2 tbsp. tomato ketchup

2 tbsp. tomato concentrate

1 Oxo cube

2 tbsp. pine nuts

Vegetable oil and butter for cooking

Salt & pepper

Method

Soften the onion in some butter, add the vegetables, pine nuts and garlic and fry, stirring regularly, until cooked. Set aside. Fry the meat for a minute or two until it starts to turn brown and then remove as much fat as possible. Add the Worcestershire sauce, tomato ketchup, tomato concentrate and crumbled oxo cube and continue to fry, stirring regularly until the meat is cooked. Combine with the onion mixture and set aside until needed. Cut the marrow into 2 to 3 inch thick slices and scoop out the seeds in the centre. If the marrow is old, peel the slices before cooking. Place the rings in a greased ovenproof dish and bake in the oven for 7 or 8 minutes. Turn the rings over carefully and bake for a further 7 or 8 minutes until they are cooked. Spoon the meat mixture into the centre of each ring and heat in the oven for 5 or 10 minutes and serve.

Meat Loaf

For some reason, Americans lay claim to this simple dish. Why they should feel it was created over there is hard to understand. There is no doubt, however, that it is extremely popular all over the States and I have included a recipe here that was given to me by a keen and earnest American foodie. The exciting thing about the American attitude to their meat loaf is that anything goes. You can add and adjust the ingredients to suit your taste; chilli sauce, Worcestershire sauce, mustard powder or even different meats such as chicken or tinned corned beef.

To serve 6 – 8

1 lb minced beef

1 lb minced pork

3 cloves garlic, finely chopped

3 onions, finely chopped

3 stalks celery, finely chopped

2 carrots, peeled and finely diced

$1/4$ pint red wine

4 slices brown bread

2 eggs well beaten

$1/2$ tsp. each thyme, oregano and marjoram

2 crushed bay leaves

2 tbsp. olive oil

2 tbsp. Worcestershire sauce

2 tbsp. tomato concentrate

2 tbsp. butter

Pinch of allspice

Salt & freshly ground black pepper

Method

Sweat the onions, celery and garlic in the oil until they become translucent. Pour in the wine and simmer for a few moments to warm. Cut the crusts off the bread, dice and add to the wine mixture and pour the lot over the minced meat in a mixing bowl. Add the spices and all other ingredients, including the beaten eggs, and mix well. Spoon the mixture into a well greased loaf tin, cover with tinfoil and bake in a medium oven for about an hour. If desired, after about 45 minutes remove the tinfoil in order to brown the top. Serve, hot or cold, with tomato or chilli sauce, salad and boiled potatoes.

Beef Olives

To serve 4 – 6

1 $1/2$ – 2 lb topside of beef

1 onion, finely chopped

4 egg yolks, hard boiled

5 tbsp. breadcrumbs

1 egg, well beaten

2 tsp. parsley, finely chopped

1 tbsp. shredded suet

$1/2$ tsp. ground ginger

$1/2$ tsp. turmeric powder

Pinch of mixed dried herbs

1 tsp. grated lemon rind

Butter

1 cup of beef stock

Salt & freshly ground black pepper

Cider vinegar

Method

Slice the beef against the grain into at least six slices. Beat each piece flat and as thin as possible without shredding the meat. Mix the onion, egg yolks, breadcrumbs, beaten egg, parsley, suet, lemon rind and all spices and herbs in a blender until well kneaded.

Season well and then divide the stuffing into as many portions as you have beef slices and spread over the meat. Roll them up like small Swiss rolls and secure with wooden toothpicks or tie with string. Lay the olives, side by side, cut-edge down in a casserole and dot with butter. Pour over the beef stock and bake in a hot oven for 30 minutes, turning once. Lay the olives on a serving dish, sprinkle with the vinegar and garnish with more chopped parsley and a little paprika and serve hot with peas and mashed or boiled potatoes.

Bollito Misto

Bollito misto is a boiled meat speciality which originated in Piedmont, Northern Italy. The name of the dish simply means 'boiled mixed'. The Italians believe the vegetables used should include a selection which represent the colours of the Italian flag – red, white and green. I have chosen a selection of meat, pickled cabbage, carrots and boiled potatoes. You cannot beat this dish as a lunchtime cure for a heavy night of overindulgence and it compares favourably with our English hotpot or the New England boiled dinner.

To serve 4 – 8

2 lb salted tongue

2 lb rump of veal or if unavailable, pork

4 lb chicken

2 lb joint of beef (brisket or shin)

1 salami or cotechino sausage

3 onions, quartered

3 carrots, chopped

3 sticks of celery chopped

Bouquet garni

Salt and pepper

Method

Place the tongue in a pot of cold water and bring to the boil and then drain, discarding the water. Place the onions, carrots, celery and bouquet garni in the pot, cover the tongue and vegetables with cold water, bring to the boil and simmer gently for an hour. Add the beef and veal and cook for another hour. Keep an eye on the pot and skim any froth that forms on the surface. Remove the tongue from the pot and set aside. Put in the well-seasoned chicken and cook for at least half an hour. In the mean time, once the tongue is cool enough to handle, trim the base and peel off the skin. Return it to the pot and cook for a further 45 minutes. 20 minutes before the meat is cooked, add the sausage and boil for 20 minutes. When all is cooked, lift out the meats and carve a few slices for each individual and arrange in a big dish with some of the cooking liquor to keep the meat moist. Serve with carrots, pickled cabbage and boiled potatoes.

Pickled cabbage

Shred half a cored cabbage and boil it in some olive oil with a tin of plum tomatoes. Add a little sugar, salt and pepper and simmer for 20 minutes, stirring occasionally. Once cooked, stir in half a cup of white wine vinegar and boil rapidly. Remove from the heat and rest. Reheat and serve with the bollito and a few pickled onions, capers or gherkins.

Wichnor Manor and the Flitch of Bacon

I have become fascinated by stories of ancient customs related to food in villages hundreds of years ago. Why did the customs start and who started them?

In 1338, as an example, Wichnor manor was held by Sir Philip de Somerville under John of Gaunt, Duke of Lancaster, who, when staying at nearby Tutbury Castle, established several curious customs. One of the most bizarre concerned a flitch of bacon. The Duke insisted that it should be hung in the hall at Wichnor all year round, except in Lent, so that any man or woman could claim it if they had been married for a year and a day without quarrelling or repenting. Two people had to testify to the truth of the claim but if the claimant was a freeman, he received, besides the bacon, half a quarter of wheat and a cheese, but if he was a serf, he only got half a quarter of rye.

A grand procession was organized through the village, the bacon and other things leading the way, carried aloft by minstrels with trumpets and tabernets, the tenants following as the worthy couple returned to their house.

Very few people dared to claim the prize once the custom was established, but one couple who did argued about how to cook the bacon so were asked to return it. Another couple, a sailor and his wife, had never seen each other since the day of their marriage. Latterly, a simple couple – the husband a good-natured sort and the wife luckily dumb, claimed the prize.

No claimant for the flitch appeared for many years after that and, as a result, a wooden one was substituted and hangs there still; a reminder, if it were necessary, for young married couples to be wary of trusting themselves in the hymeneal noose.

CHAPTER SIX

PORK & HAM

Years ago, most Devon farmers kept a sow or two for their own use and, just before Christmas, one would be slaughtered and butchered on the farm. Just about every part of a pig was eaten in some way or another. The head was stripped of its meat and made into brawn, the hams and gammons were salted and hung for smoking. They produced the fat bacon with little lean so beloved of Devonians. The intestines were cleaned and fried with onions to make 'chitterlings' and lard was produced from the fat of the stomach. Pork is the best value meat in the shops or from farmers markets at the moment.

Suckling Pig

It is almost impossible to find a regular supplier of suckling pigs. Farmers argue that most profit is made on pigs matured from weaners and it is pointless them selling the piglets too early. Some research and a good deal of kow-towing to a local butcher may be the answer, but make sure your oven is large enough to take the pig. They weigh between 15 – 25 lbs and are rarely shorter than 20 inches in length. The best suckling pig we have eaten was cooked on an open fire in our local pub, the 'Northmore Arms' at Wonson, near Chagford in Devon.

To serve up to 12

16 lb suckling pig

Stuffing

5 fillets of pork (enough to fill the cavity)

3 oz. flat-leaved parsley

3 oz. coarsely chopped fennel

1 tbsp. chopped rosemary

3 cloves garlic, finely chopped

2 lemons sliced

Salt and pepper

Marinade

1 pint red wine

1/4 cup vinegar

1/2 cup olive oil

4 cloves garlic, crushed

4 bay leaves, crushed

4 or 5 cloves, bruised

Pepper

Method

Rub the marinade into the meat inside and out and leave in the mixture for several hours, turning regularly. When you are ready to cook it, turn the pig on its back and stuff the cavity with the fillets of pork, and the other stuffing ingredients mixed together. Sew up the flaps, bind the pig with string and place on a greased rack in a hot oven dish. Cook in a slow oven 180°c for at least three hours, basting regularly with oil. Turn it over once to ensure it is brown and crisp on both sides. When cooked, remove the pig and allow it to stand for 15 minutes or so. Skim the fat from the juices in the tray, reduce, check seasoning and use as a sauce. A stuffed pig of this size is more than enough for a dinner for 12 people. Serve with apple sauce.

Sliced Ham in Leek and Cream Sauce

This is one of our staples and is good 'Fat boy' food. It is ideal for a dinner party as it can be prepared a day or two before and slapped in the oven when required. The ingredients can be varied according to taste but, we like it with Gruyere cheese and probably too much vermouth. It is an excellent way of dealing with leftover ham after Christmas.

To serve 6 – 8

4 lb piece of smoked ham

2 lb leeks

2 tbsp. plain flour

1 pint milk

4 oz. butter

8 fl. oz. double cream

3 oz. Gruyere cheese, grated

8 fl. oz. dry vermouth or very dry sherry

Salt & pepper

Method

Wash and clean the leeks and slice finely. Melt the butter in a large pan and stew the leeks until very tender. Add the flour and milk, stirring continuously. Add the vermouth and stir to form a smooth paste. Simmer gently for half an hour or so, add the cream and cheese and continue to stir until dissolved. Check the seasoning and pour half the mixture into a suitable ovenware dish. Carve the ham into thick slices and lay them, overlapping, on the mixture. Pour the rest of the mixture over the ham and either keep in the fridge until required or heat in the oven for 10 minutes or so. Serve with new potatoes. Delicious!

Jambalaya

Creole jambalaya from New Orleans has evolved with a mix of French, Spanish, Indian and Afro-Caribbean culinary influences. It takes some time to prepare and cook but the result is worth the effort.

To serve 6 – 8

1 lb tiger prawns, shelled

1 lb cooked ham, cut into 1 inch squares

$1/2$ lb chorizo sausage, sliced (garlic sausage if chorizo is not available)

5 tomatoes peeled, seeded and chopped

2 tbsp. tomato concentrate

1 onion, finely chopped

1 green pepper, finely chopped

1 celery stalk, finely chopped

$3/4$ lb risotto rice

$1/2$ tsp. each oregano, thyme and ground cloves

4 cloves garlic, sliced

4 tbsp. olive oil

4 tbsp. butter

2 pints chicken stock

1 glass sherry

Handful of chopped parsley

Salt & pepper

1 tsp. chilli powder

Method

Fry the ham chunks and sausage slices in the olive oil until they begin to turn brown. In an oven proof casserole, sweat the chopped onion in the butter until transparent, pour in the rice and stir gently until the rice begins to colour. Add the ham and sausage mixture, stir in the chopped celery, pepper, tomatoes, chilli powder and tomato concentrate. Add the seasoning, garlic and herbs. In a separate pot, bring the chicken stock to the boil and pour over the jambalaya mixture, cover the casserole and simmer for 30 minutes or so until the rice is tender. Add the prawns 5 minutes before the rice is cooked. Add more liquid if necessary. Remove from the heat, add the sherry and a handful of parsley, check the seasoning and serve hot.

Ham Terrine

A classic summer lunchtime staple which can be prepared days in advance and kept in the fridge.

To serve 4 – 6

2 unsmoked ham knuckles, soaked in water for 24 hours

2 pints chicken stock

2 onions, thickly sliced

2 carrots, cut into chunks

1 stick celery, cut into chunks

1 sprig of fresh oregano

4 leeks, cleaned and trimmed

1 sprig of fresh rosemary

2 sheets of gelatine

Salt & pepper

Method

Place the knuckles in a large pot and pour in the stock, chopped vegetables and herbs, add sufficient water to ensure that the meat is covered and bring slowly to the boil. Remove from the heat and simmer gently for 3 hours in the bottom oven of an Aga or in a slow oven. Put in the leeks when there is about $1/2$ hour of cooking time left. When the meat is cooked, allow it to stand in the cooking juices. When cool enough to handle, remove the knuckles and strain the liquid and season. Discard the vegetable chunks but save the leeks. If necessary, the liquid can be reduced to increase the flavour. Dissolve the gelatine in about a pint of the liquid and cool. Take the meat from the bones, removing most of the fat and all the skin and shred the meat into fibres. Line a 1lb baking tin with clingfilm and place some of the meat in the bottom covered by some of the liquid. Leave in the fridge to set for a minute or two then put in a row of leeks, cut to fit the tin and cover with more of the liquid. Repeat the layers until all the meat and leeks are used up. Cover with more clingfilm and leave in the fridge for a day to set. To serve, dip the tin briefly into a bowl of warm water, turn upside down and slide the tureen onto a serving plate and cut into slices.

Stuffed Pigs Trotters

A number of famous chefs have created recipes for this dish but I have tried to keep this one as simple as possible. Ask your butcher to bone the trotters (back legs only) as the process is tricky. Tell him to cut the skin from the ankle to the top on the underside of each trotter in order to remove the bones. Be careful to avoid puncturing the skins elsewhere as they will be used to form sausage skins.

To serve 4

4 pig's trotters

1 onion, carrot and celery stalk, roughly chopped

1 pint beef stock

$1/2$ bottle white wine

Salt & freshly ground black pepper

For the filling

8 oz. chicken breast (skinned)

1 onion, finely chopped

1 egg

$1/2$ tsp. ground nutmeg

1 tbsp. ground or finely chopped fresh ginger

8 fl. oz. double cream

2 tbsp. raisins

Salt & white pepper

For the sauce

1 pint chicken stock

1 onion or 2 shallots, finely chopped

10 cloves garlic, finely chopped

$1/2$ pint Madeira

$1/4$ pint water

6 dried morels

Method

Fry the onion, carrot and celery in some olive oil in a casserole dish for a minute or two, add the trotters and the wine and boil until the wine is reduced by half. Add the stock and bring to the boil and place in a hot oven for 3 hours, ensuring that the liquid covers the trotters. Remove the trotters from the juice and allow to cool. To prepare the filling, place all the ingredients, except the raisins, in a food processor and blend to a paste. Add the raisins and mix well. Season with salt and white pepper and allow to cool. To make the sauce, fry the onions and garlic in a deep frying pan until they turn golden. Add the chicken stock and water and bring to the boil. Simmer on medium heat and reduce by half. Add the Madeira and continue to reduce until the sauce begins to thicken. Add a knob of butter and adjust the seasoning. Using a fine sieve, strain the sauce, which should be rich and thick enough to coat the back of a spoon. To stuff the trotters, cut out four squares of tinfoil large enough to completely wrap the trotters and butter on one side. Lay each trotter on the tinfoil, skin side down and divide the filling into 4 equal amounts. Stuff each trotter to form its original shape, with the cut side down and wrap in the tinfoil. Twist the ends to secure the parcels. Poach the trotters in a large pan of boiling water for 30 minutes and serve with the warmed sauce and some mashed or boiled potatoes.

Pork Terrine

The most important domestic animal in a farmer's yard was the pig. Their wives had more ways of preparing and preserving the meat of the animal, slaughtered in the autumn, than any other. This recipe has to be the simplest and cheapest pate to make and offers plenty of opportunity for personalising.

To serve 4

3/4 lbs minced pork belly

1/2 lb streaky bacon

1 1/2 lbs spinach (new season is best)

1 onion, finely diced

2 cloves garlic, chopped

1 wine glass of cooking brandy or Madeira

3 chicken livers, finely chopped

2 tbsp. of mixed chopped nuts

1 egg, beaten

Butter for frying

Spices

1/4 tsp. ground cloves

1/4 tsp. ground allspice

1/4 tsp. grated nutmeg

Salt and black pepper

Method

Cook the spinach in a small amount of boiling water for a minute or so and then remove, drain and squeeze out as much liquid as possible. Chop finely and leave to drain in a colander. Fry the onion and garlic in some butter until soft and mix with the spinach. Stretch the bacon with the back of a knife and line a 2 lb bread tin, leaving sufficient overhang to cover the top when the filling is in place. Blend the spinach mixture, nuts, belly pork and chopped liver in a large bowl and add the spices and beaten egg, ensuring it is well mixed. Flavour with plenty of salt, pepper and brandy. Pack the mixture into the bread tin, ensuring it reaches all the corners and fold over the bacon. Cover with foil and place the tin in baking dish half filled with hot water. Bake in the top of an Aga or hot oven for at least 1 1/2 hours. When cooked through, remove the tin and allow it to cool slightly. When cool enough to handle, place a weighted board on top and leave to cool further until it can be stored in the refrigerator. It is best left overnight to allow the flavours to blend. Remove the pate from its tin and wrap in clingfilm and tinfoil. Store in the fridge for a couple of days or freeze until required. Slice thickly and serve with pickles as a starter or light supper.

Sweet & Sour Pork & Prawn Balls

This dish can be made with prawns, shrimps or any firm white fish such as coley or cod.

To serve 4
For the meat balls

4 oz. minced pork

1 lb peeled prawns

1 tbsp. light soy sauce

2 tbsp. water

1 tbsp. cornflour

1 tbsp. dry sherry or Chinese rice wine

1 tsp. sugar

1/2 tsp. salt

Oil for frying

1 tbsp. plain flour

For the batter

8 tsp. flour, sieved

8 tbsp. ice-cold water

1 egg

For the sweet and sour sauce

1/4 pint pineapple juice

1 tbsp. vegetable oil

1 tbsp. cornstarch

3 tbsp. vinegar

2 tbsp. water

2 tbsp. brown sugar

3 tbsp. soy sauce

Method

Pound pork and prawns into a paste in a bowl with all the other meat ingredients except the flour. Form into balls the size of walnuts, roll in the flour to make handling easier and set aside. Stir the egg in a bowl without beating, add the iced water and keep stirring, shake in the sieved flour and mix to form a batter. Heat the oil in a wok or deep frying pan, dip the meat balls in the batter and place carefully in the oil in the wok and fry for about 5 minutes, turning from time to time, until golden on all sides. Drain, place in a serving bowl and keep warm. Mix the cornflour, oil, water, sugar, soy sauce and vinegar together and place in a small pan. Stir in the pineapple juice and heat for 4 or 5 minutes until the juice begins to thicken, stirring constantly. Pour over the pork and prawn balls and serve hot with boiled or fried rice.

Choucroute

I didn't know where to put this recipe, it should, I suppose, fit in amongst the vegetables, but with the enormous selection of meats involved, it seemed out of place, so here it is. The sight of a steaming dish of new season pickled cabbage surrounded by a selection of spicy sausages and other meats is a truly 'Fat boy' delight in the autumn.

Nobody can agree where the finest choucroute comes from, is it from France, Belgium or Germany? They are, of course, related but knowing how chauvinistic the French are in their belief that everything to do with food and its preparation cannot be bettered anywhere else in the world, I reluctantly suggest the original recipe probably comes from Alsace.

To serve 4 and it isn't worth preparing it for less

2 lb jar of choucroute or sauerkraut, drained

4 frankfurters

1 lb boneless smoked pork loin

1/2 lb smoked ham

1/4 lb piece unsliced bacon

4 spicy fresh pork sausages

4 smoked pork sausages

2 blood sausages (in the round if possible)

2 onions, finely sliced

1/2 bottle Alsace Riesling or other fruity white wine

Bouquet garni, to consist of:
1/2 tsp. each juniper berries, peppercorns, cloves and 5 cloves of garlic, peeled and bruised

8 small potatoes, peeled

4 oz. lard or butter

Salt & freshly ground pepper

Method

Melt the lard in a large heavy pan and sweat the onions. Pour in the wine, add the bouquet garni and simmer for a few minutes. Add the choucroute, pork loin, ham and bacon and cook for about 3 hours. Ten minutes before serving, add the fresh and smoked pork sausages and the blood sausages. Boil the potatoes in salted water until cooked, drain and keep warm. Remove the sausages from the choucroute and fry in a little oil until brown on all sides. To serve, remove all the meat and cut into portions. Remove and discard the bouquet garni, drain the choucroute and pile into the centre of a serving dish. Surround with the sausages and meat and, lastly, the potatoes and serve.

Boiled Gammon with Pease Pudding

This is another classic 'Fat boy' special. It is easy to cook and is delicious hot or cold. I discovered that pease pudding is one of the oldest dishes in English cookery and was made originally from dried green peas or even old fresh peas with their skins on.

To serve 6

For the Pease Pudding

1 lb split peas, soaked overnight

1 shallot or small onion, finely chopped

Mixed bunch of herbs to include – mint, thyme, marjoram and parsley, tied together

2 oz. butter

Salt and freshly ground black pepper

For the Gammon

3 lb piece of gammon

2 onions, each studded with cloves

2 carrots, peeled and roughly chopped

2 sticks of celery, roughly chopped

2 or 3 bay leaves

6 peppercorns

Method

Place the meat in a large pan, cover with cold water and slowly bring to the boil. Remove the meat and discard the water. Cover the gammon with fresh cold water and add the rest of the ingredients and, again, slowly bring to the boil. Tie the ingredients for the pease pudding in a piece of muslin and place in the boiling liquid. Skim off any scum that rises to the surface, cover and simmer on low heat for at least 3 hours until the meat is very tender. Remove the muslin bag, discard the herbs and mash the peas and butter, season well and keep warm in a small bowl on the stove. Remove the meat from the liquid and carve into thick slices. Some of the cooking liquor can be used as gravy. Serve with a couple of spoonfuls of pease pudding, boiled carrots or sprouts and boiled potatoes for a really filling meal.

Pork Medallions with Garlic and Lemon

This dish can be made as easily using chicken breasts instead of fillet of pork but I feel the texture of the pork makes for a more satisfying meal and seems to gel better with the garlic and lemon. Simple to make and delicious with boiled new potatoes.

To serve 4

2 fillets of pork (tenderloin) weight approx. 1 $1/2$ lbs

1 tbsp. olive oil

3 cloves garlic, finely chopped

2 oz. butter

Juice of 1 lemon

Salt & black pepper

Method

Remove all skin, fat and membrane from the fillets and chop diagonally into $1/2$ inch discs. Place each disc between cling film and batter flat. Season well with salt and pepper. In a heavy pan, heat the oil and about $1/4$ of the butter until very and fry the discs on one side until golden, turn them over, adding the garlic, and fry until sealed. Add the rest of the butter in lumps and continue to fry until the pork is cooked. Add more seasoning. Remove the meat to a serving dish, continue to fry the garlic until it starts to turn golden then add the lemon juice, remove from the heat and pour the juices over the pork medallions and serve.

Keuls 04

A Brief History of the Genus Capsicum

Chilli peppers are perennial subshrubs native to South America but grown as annuals in colder parts of the world. There are over twenty-five species of capsicum ranging from the mild bell to the hottest habanero chilli pepper. They are all members of the solanaceae family, which includes aubergine, tomato, potato and tobacco plants but not the black pepper used in pepper grinders, known to botanists as *piper nigrum*. First cultivation of the plant is thought to have taken place around 7000 BC in an area around Huaca Prieta in Peru. The chilli pepper arrived in India, probably in Goa, with the Portuguese in about 1490 and its popularity as a spice ingredient was rapidly spread throughout South East Asia. The sweet pepper, on the other hand, was better suited to the Mediterranean climate and its introduction into southern Europe came directly through the Spanish and Portuguese who brought them over from their new colonies in South America. The heat in chillies comes from a substance known as capsaicin, manufactured in the placenta, the central core of the fruit. From here, pungency is transmitted to the seeds and outer skin. Removal of the seeds and central core of the chilli before cooking reduces the pungency, therefore. The flavour of a chilli comes from aromatic compounds in the outer skin. Even very hot chillies can have a very distinctive taste and this may explain why some cooks recommend keeping some chillies whole in the cooking process. As a general rule, the smaller and more pointed a chilli is the more pungent it will tend to be. Colour on the other hand is not a factor of hotness.

CHAPTER SEVEN

CURRY

Well here we are at last – the curry section! I could, and maybe will one day, write a book simply about curry. But on this occasion I have decided to include recipes for a selection of South Indian curries, a biriyani and one or two Thai recipes. A meal could include all or a selection of these dishes and the amount of chilli used can be varied according to personal taste. A curry does not have to be hot to be good but the curry powder or spice blend (masala) is better made with freshly ground spices.

Few people in India would recognize some of the names used to describe curries in this Country, for example, Chicken Madras means little to people in, what is now, Tamil Nadu and Rogan Josh simply means 'red juice'. England's favourite curries, Chicken Tikka Masala and Chicken Korma are meaningless outside the lager swilling laddish communities of our major cities. Vindaloo, a name used to describe the hottest Indian curry, probably comes from the Portuguese words, vinho (wine) and ahlos (garlic) to describe the dish developed by the Portuguese in Goa. It consisted originally of pork pickled in vinegar and a blend of very hot spices.

In Kerala, the rice used is not, surprisingly, basmati, but a local, chunkier rice with rounded grains, rather like the rice used by Italians to make risotto. The curries should be served at the same time in small dishes with the rice on the side and a tart lemon or lime pickle or chutney. It is impossible to state the definitive ingredients for any curry. In India there are as many recipes as there are religions, languages and states. I have chosen to include those which require ingredients easily obtainable over here. First of all, however, one needs to prepare the spice powders (masalas). In Kerala there are only three basic ones.

Garam Masala

Garam masala, which means hot mixture, is the base for most Indian vegetable dishes and is made from a mixture of several spices ground together. There are many versions but you should mix and match and make your own special blend. It is best prepared in small quantities and kept in airtight jars. It loses its potency rapidly, so a new batch should be made regularly. One can, of course, buy ready-made garam masala in most stores now, but nothing beats the home-made version.

1 tbsp. black cumin seeds

1 tbsp. white cumin seeds

2 tbsp. coriander seeds

1 tsp. brown cardamom seeds (husks removed)

4 dried bay leaves

1 tsp. cloves

1 tbsp. black peppercorns

1 whole nutmeg, grated

1 inch cinnamon stick

Method
Place all the ingredients in an ovenproof dish and dry roast them in a low oven for a few minutes until they give off a strong aromatic smell. Grind all the spices, bit by bit, in an electric grinder or by hand in pestle and mortar. Store in a sealed jar.

Sambar Masala

This spice powder is used prolifically in South India, usually for cooking chicken.

Prepare as above
1 tsp. fenugreek seeds

1 tbsp. coriander seeds

15 black peppercorns

2 tsp. each white mustard seeds and white cumin seeds

2 tsp. turmeric powder

6 dried red chillies

Fish Masala

Prepare as above
7 cloves

4 brown cardamoms (remove husks)

1 inch cinnamon stick

1 tbsp. each, turmeric powder, white and black cumin seeds

3 tbsp. coriander seeds

8 dried red chillies

2 tsp. fenugreek seeds

Kolambi (Prawn) Curry

To serve 4 – 6

20-25 medium sized prawns

2 medium-sized onions, finely chopped

1 tomato skinned, deseeded and chopped

1 peeled potato, cut into small cubes

Spices

$1/2$ tsp. fresh ginger, mashed into a paste

1 tsp. garlic, mashed into a paste

1 tsp. fish masala

1 tsp. red chilli powder (optional)

1 tsp. turmeric powder

1 tbsp. tamarind juice

Finely chopped coriander leaves for garnish.

Salt & pepper

Method

Mix the turmeric, salt and half the chilli powder in a bowl, clean the prawns and add them to the mixture to marinate for 20 minutes or so. Sweat the chopped onions in butter until soft. Add the fish masala and rest of the red chilli powder. Add the potato cubes along with some salt and pepper and the ginger and garlic pastes. Sauté on low heat until the potato pieces are cooked. Add the tomatoes and continue to stir gently. Gently fry the mixture until all the spices are well blended. Add the prawns and the marinade, cover with a lid and cook on low heat. When the prawns are cooked, add the tamarind juice and garnish with coriander leaves and freshly grated coconut. The result should be dry and spicy.

Malay Lamb Curry

To serve 4 – 6

1 lb leg of lamb, cut into 1 inch cubes

2 onions, finely chopped

1 tbsp. ground coriander

3 garlic cloves, crushed

2 tsp. grated ginger

2 tsp. turmeric powder

1 tbsp. concentrated tamarind juice or 2 tbsp. lime juice

$1/2$ tsp. ground cumin

$1/2$ tsp. ground black pepper

1 tsp. each of salt and freshly ground black pepper

1 tsp. chilli powder

4 or more green chillies, sliced

1 tin coconut milk or 4 oz solid coconut cream

1 tin chopped tomatoes

Vegetable oil for cooking

Method

Mix one of the chopped onions, the garlic, ginger and powdered turmeric, cumin, salt and pepper and chilli powder in a bowl. Coat the lamb with the mixture and leave covered in the fridge overnight. Heat some oil in a heavy pot and sweat the other chopped onion, add the lamb with the marinade and stir-fry until well browned. Add the tomato and coconut and bring to the boil. Reduce heat and simmer for 30 minutes or so until the sauce thickens. Stir in the chillies and continue to simmer until the meat is tender and most of the liquid has evaporated. It is better to cook the curry the day before it is required and to reheat it before serving.

Kerala Fried Fish

To serve 4

1 lb fish fillets (coley, cod or any other white fish)

2 tsp. red chilli powder (optional)

2 tsp. fish masala

$1/2$ tsp. turmeric powder

1 inch ginger, grated

1 tsp. ground black pepper

1 tsp. vinegar

Salt and oil for frying

Method

Clean and wipe the fish and cut into 4 inch pieces. Make a paste of the ginger, pepper, chilli and turmeric powder, salt and vinegar. Add a few teaspoons of water to make a thick, smooth paste. Apply the paste to both sides of the fish slices in a very thin layer. Allow to marinate for 45 minutes or longer. Fry the fish pieces until golden brown and serve with lime and onion slices.

South Indian Chicken Curry

To serve 4

1 lb chicken thighs, boned, skinned and cubed

2 tbsp. oil

1 onion finely chopped

1 tbsp. each of chopped ginger and garlic

3 tomatoes

1 tbsp. sambhar masala

8 fl. oz. coconut cream

Salt

Method

Heat the oil in a deep pan and sweat the chopped onion until soft. Blitz the garlic and ginger with the sambar masala to form a paste. Add the paste to the pan and fry gently over low heat, stirring constantly until the oil begins to separate. Add the tomatoes and stir for a few minutes until the tomatoes break up, add the cubed chicken and some salt and mix well. If the sauce is too thick add a drop or two of water. Cook over a medium heat for 5 minutes.

Pour in the coconut cream and bring to the boil and simmer for 20 minutes until the chicken is cooked. Serve with boiled rice. The result should be dry and hot. Do not overcook the chicken as it may become tough.

Sambhar
(Vegetable Curry)

To serve 4

4 oz. dal

3 tbsp. sambhar masala

1/2 lb lady's fingers, cut into small pieces

2 onion, chopped

2 potatoes, peeled and cut into small pieces

1 large aubergine, chopped into cubes

1 tbsp. chopped coriander leaves

1 tsp. chopped garlic

2 dried red chillies, cut into pieces

Salt

2 tomatoes, skinned, deseeded and chopped

1/2 cup diluted tamarind or lime juice

1 tsp. black mustard seeds

Vegetable oil

Method

Boil the dal in two cups of water, when almost cooked, add the potato, aubergine, lady's fingers, onion, tomato and salt. Continue to cook until the dal becomes soft. Dissolve sambhar masala in a little water and add it to the cooked vegetables. Add the diluted tamarind juice and blend well. In another pan, heat oil and add mustard seeds. When they stop spluttering, add chopped garlic and the dried red chilli pieces. Fry for two minutes and then add to the dal and vegetable mixture and simmer on low heat for a few minutes. Finally, add chopped coriander leaves on the top. Serve hot with paraunthas or chapatis.

Chicken Biriyani

To serve 4 – 6

1 lb basmati rice

8 chicken pieces – drumsticks and thighs

1 onion, sliced lengthways

1 oz. cashew nuts

1 oz. raisins

2 green chillies, thinly sliced lengthways

Curry leaves or coriander leaves

1^1/$_2$ pints hot water

Butter for cooking

Salt and freshly ground black pepper

Paste mixture

2 inch ginger, peeled and chopped fine

1 onion, finely chopped

1 tsp. garam masala

4 cloves garlic, crushed

Salt and freshly ground black pepper

Spices

1 inch cinnamon stick

3 green cardamom

1 brown cardamom, crushed

4 whole cloves

^{1}/$_2$ tsp. coriander powder

^{1}/$_2$ tsp. turmeric powder

1 tsp. chilli powder

6 black peppercorns

Method

Fry the cashew nuts and raisins for a minute or two in butter and reserve for garnish. Sauté the sliced onion until golden and reserve half for garnish, together with the sliced green chillies and curry leaves. Grind the paste ingredients until smooth and rub the mixture onto the chicken bits. Leave to stand for an hour or two. Add the spices to the other half of the sauteed sliced onion, stir-fry using more butter if required, for a minute or two then add the chicken and continue to cook for 15 or 20 minutes until well browned. Add the rice and mix well. Shake the pan to ensure that all the grains are coated and it begins to splutter. Add the hot water, season with salt and pepper and cook on low heat for a further 20 minutes. Add more hot water if necessary and continue cooking until all the water is absorbed and the rice is cooked. Place the rice in an ovenproof dish and layer with the chicken. Bake at a low temperature for 10 minutes and serve hot. Garnish with the fried onion, cashews, chillies, curry leaves and raisins and pour over a little melted butter.

Thai Curry

Thai curries are made using one of three basic pastes – red, green or yellow but, unlike Indian and African curry dishes, the curries are water based and, as a result, appear to have a cleaner, less greasy taste. It is usual for the green curry to be used with chicken, the red with fish and beef and the yellow with pork, but there appears to be no firm and fast rule in this regard. It is much better to make the paste freshly each time by grinding the ingredients down with a little oil to form a thick paste. The ingredients for each paste recipe provide enough to make one curry to feed four people. Needless to say all these curry pastes are now readily available in the shops, ready mixed.

Green Curry Paste

2 tbsp. chopped red bell pepper

2 tbsp. chopped carrot

8 red chillies

1 tsp. fish sauce

2 tsp. paprika

1 inch ginger, finely sliced

1 tsp. cumin seed

1 tsp. coriander seed

1 stalk lemon grass, chopped

1/2 tsp. shrimp paste

4 cloves garlic

6 chopped shallots

Vegetable oil

Yellow Curry Paste

2 tbsp. chopped yellow bell pepper

1 tsp. ground turmeric powder

8 red chillies

1 inch ginger, finely sliced

1/2 tsp. ground coriander

1/2 tsp. ground cumin

1 stalk chopped lemon grass

1 tsp. fish sauce

1 tsp. shrimp paste

6 chopped shallots

1 tbsp. fresh basil

Vegetable oil

Red Curry Paste

2 tbsp. chopped green bell pepper

8 green chillies

1 stalk lemon grass, chopped

1 inch ginger, finely sliced

1/2 tsp. ground coriander seeds

1/2 tsp. shrimp paste

Vegetable oil

1 tbsp. chopped fresh coriander

1 tsp. fish sauce

4 cloves garlic

1/2 tsp. ground cumin

6 chopped shallots

Bunch of spring onions

Thai Green Chicken Curry
(Gaeng Kheow Wan Gai)

To serve 4 – 6

8 Chicken thighs, boned and cut into bite-sized pieces

Green curry paste, prepared as above

1/2 pint coconut milk

2 tbsp. fish sauce

Juice of 1 lemon

1 cup pea aubergines, or 1 medium aubergine chopped into small squares

Few pieces of dried white & black fungus (Muc Nhi Hay)

Handful chopped basil for garnish

Vegetable oil for cooking

1/2 pint water

Method

Soak the white black fungus in a little water until it trebles in size and becomes soft. Shred into bite-sized pieces and put aside. Heat the oil in a wok or large pan and stir-fry the green curry paste for a moment or two to release the aroma. Add the water and coconut milk and stir for a few minutes to allow the coconut milk to thicken. Add the fish sauce, aubergine, white black fungus and the chicken. Cook over a medium heat until the chicken is almost cooked and add the lemon juice and half the chopped basil. Continue to simmer, stirring regularly and when all is cooked through, remove from the heat and serve immediately with the balance of the chopped basil sprinkled on top.

Spiced Persian Lamb Curry
(Lamb Dhansak)

To serve 4 – 6

1 lb cubed, boned shoulder of lamb

1 lb split red lentils

I onion, finely chopped

4 bay leaves

2 tsp. each of ground coriander and cumin

1 cinnamon stick

Butter

2 tbsp. tamarind pulp or 3 tbsp. lime juice

1 tsp. turmeric

6 cloves

1 tsp. fenugreek seeds

3 cloves garlic, finely chopped

2 tsp. chopped fresh ginger

2 hot red chillies

6 squashed cardamom pods

Olive oil

Method

Soak the lentils in boiling water for 15 minutes and then drain and mix with the cinnamon, coriander, turmeric, bay leaves and the chillies in a saucepan. Cover with water, bring to the boil and then simmer for 1/2 an hour until the lentils are tender. Remove the whole spices and the bay leaves and mash the lentils to a puree. Put the cumin, cardamom and fenugreek seeds in a blender with the onion, garlic and ginger and blend to a paste. Put some oil and butter in a heavy casserole and brown the lamb chunks all over before adding the paste. Stir to ensure that all the lamb pieces are coated with the mixture. Add just enough water to cover, add a pinch or two of salt and simmer for 45 – 55 minutes until the meat is tender. Soak the tamarind pulp in hot water to extract the juice (or use limejuice) and add to the stew with the lentil puree. Serve with couscous or boiled rice and lime pickle.

CHAPTER EIGHT

PULSES, GRAINS, PASTA AND NOODLES

Dried beans of one type or another, with bones and bacon to flavour them, are the staple peasant food of all Mediterranean countries. It was only after the discovery of the New World that a replacement for the dried broad bean was discovered, but now pulses of all sorts are in common use. I have included a few ideas for preparing classic bean stews found in Spain and France, which come with a variety of names and ingredients. Try one and then adjust the ingredients to suit your taste and the availability of the produce. I have also included recipes for dishes using noodles, pasta or rice from different parts of the world, all of which have one thing in common – simplicity.

Bean and Pork Stew

To serve 8

First stage:‑

1 lb dried white haricot beans

1 peeled onion, stuck with cloves

1 lb pork belly with the rind on

2 sliced carrots

4 cloves of garlic, crushed

Bundle of fresh herbs or tied muslin bag containing dried herbs and some peppercorns

Salt

Second stage:‑

1 duck

1 each, large smoked sausage and salami-style garlic sausage

1 lb all meat pork sausages (best choice is saucisson de Toulouse)

1 lb boned and rolled shoulder of lamb or 6 best end neck lamb chops

2 onions, chopped

1 tin of chopped tomatoes

4 cloves garlic, finely chopped

3 – 4 bay leaves

$1/2$ pint dry white wine

2 pints stock

2 handfuls of bread crumbs

1 tbsp. chopped fresh parsley

Method

Soak the beans in plenty of cold water for several hours. Rub salt in the duck inside and out and roast it on a rack in an oven roasting tin in a high oven for $1 1/2$ hours. Drain off the fat from time to time and reserve. Drain the beans, cover with lots of fresh water and bring to the boil for at least 10 minutes in a large saucepan with the rest of the ingredients in the 'first stage'. After boiling for 10 minutes, turn down the heat and simmer for at least an hour, adding more water if required. The beans at this time should be getting quite soft. Take another deep saucepan and heat the reserved duck fat. Place all the meat, apart from the duck, listed in the 'second stage' and fry until all is well browned. Remove the meat from the fat and reserve. Fry the chopped onion and $3/4$ of the garlic until browned and reserve. Save the remainder of the duck fat until the end. When the beans are cooked, remove the onion stuck with cloves and the bundle of herbs.

Cut the belly pork and the rest of the meat into large chunks and, apart from the sausages, place all the meat, tomatoes, bay leaves, wine and stock in a large pot or casserole and simmer in the oven for at least an hour. Then carve the duck into quarters and add it, together with the sausages and cook for a further $1/2$ hour until all the meat is very tender. Remove the pot from the oven and layer the meat and beans in an oven proof dish with enough of the cooking liquid to almost cover. Ensure that there is a layer of beans on top. Pour a tablespoon of the duck fat over the beans. Mix the bread crumbs, chopped parsley and the rest of the garlic and sprinkle over the beans to cover. Put the dish in a hot oven and cook for a further hour or leave in a slow oven for a couple of hours until required. The breadcrumb and bean layer will form a crust which, when cracked, releases the fragrant smell of the creamy stew below.

Cassoulet

The dish originated in the Languedoc area of France and is delicious as a filling winter 'Fat boy' meal. There are, as is often the case with peasant dishes, so many slightly different ways of preparing cassoulet. Basically, there are three types, which can be divided by the meats used. There is one from Castelnaudary which contains pork (loin, ham, leg and sausages). In Carcassone, a leg of mutton and possibly a partridge are used and finally in Toulouse, the same ingredients as Castelnaudary, but in smaller quantities with the addition of Toulouse sausage, mutton and duck or goose. Some recipes I have seen call for the addition of lamb chops but I prefer to use just duck, sometimes goose, and pork.

To serve 8 or 10 (It is not worth making it for less)

1 large duck

1 lb boned pork belly

1 lb good quality pork sausages

$1/2$ lb slab of smoked bacon, cut into large cubes

6 cloves garlic

14 oz. tin of chopped tomato

3 onions, chopped

$1/2$ pint dry white wine

1 lb dried haricot beans

$1/2$ tsp. dried thyme

3 bay leaves

3 pints chicken stock

4 slices wholemeal bread

Handful of fresh parsley

Salt & pepper

Method

Soak the beans in cold water overnight. Season the duck well and roast it on a rack in a hot oven, ensuring that the fat which drains out of the bird is collected. After about $1^{1}/2$ hours, remove the duck from the pan and keep warm. Save the duck fat until required. Drain the beans and, in a large saucepan, bring them to the boil in fresh water. Boil rapidly for at least 10 minutes, then add the bay leaves, salt and pepper and simmer for 45 minutes until they begin to soften. Check if they require more water and continue to cook until the beans are tender. Cut the pork and bacon into large squares and, together with the sausages, fry the meat in the duck fat until well browned. Remove the meat from the casserole and keep warm. Sweat the onion in the duck fat, add the garlic and continue to fry until golden. Carve the duck into joints and put all the meat into the casserole with the white wine, chicken stock, tomatoes and herbs. Check seasoning and bring to a simmer. Place in a slow oven and cook for $1^{1}/2$ hours until all the meat is cooked and tender. Put the beans into a large ovenproof dish, spoon all the meat over the beans, then the vegetables and enough of the cooking juices to come $3/4$ of the way up the dish. Process the bread and parsley in a blender and scatter the crumbs over the top. Place the dish in a low oven for about 2 hours until a crust has formed and serve hot.

Spanish Bean Stew

This dish is based on the 'cocido', so popular in various forms all over Spain. Each region will have its own variation depending to a large extent on what ingredients are available. This version is a blend that suits us and lends itself to all kinds of variations.

To serve 4 – 6

1 lb dry weight chickpeas (soaked for several hours)

1 lb selection vegetables from the garden, to include tomatoes, onions, leeks and potatoes

$1/2$ lb piece belly pork

4 oz. block of smoked bacon, cut into pieces

4 oz. black pudding, cut into $1/2$ inch discs

2 chorizo or spicy salami sausage sticks cut into $1/2$ inch lengths

1 tbsp. paprika

4 pints chicken stock

10 cloves garlic, crushed

Salt & pepper

Oil for cooking

Method

Heat the oil in a large pot and fry the garlic and bacon for a few minutes. Add the chicken stock, paprika, chickpeas, piece of pork and bring to the boil. Add a little water at this stage, if required. Simmer on gentle heat for about an hour or until the peas are almost cooked. Add the chorizo and root vegetables and continue to cook slowly. Add the green vegetables and the black pudding last. Check seasoning and serve in soup bowls with slices of warm bread.

Potato Gnocchi

The finest gnocchi dish we have eaten was enjoyed in a small family run trattoria at the unfashionable end of the Strada Nova in Venice, a city not renowned for the variety of its food. This recipe using sweet potato adds a little something special to the dish and is best eaten spread with a little melted herb butter and a good handful of grated Parmesan.

To serve 4

10 oz. sweet potato

Approximately 6 oz. plain white flour or enough to create a soft workable dough

1 egg yolk

Salt

4 oz. Parmesan, freshly grated

Method

The most important part of this recipe is that you bake the sweet potato, don't boil it. It is, of course, perfectly possible to use ordinary potatoes if you prefer but still bake them. When they are cool enough to handle, peel and mash them in a large bowl. Add the egg yolk, season with salt and mix well. Add the flour a little at a time until you have a workable dough. The trick is not to overwork the dough and to add as little flour as possible in order to end up with a lighter more tender gnocchi. Use two spoons to form the mixture into small oval shaped gnoccho and place them on a floured tray until all are prepared. Bring a large saucepan of salted water to the boil and ease the gnocchi in to the water, in batches, to simmer. Do not overcrowd the saucepan. The gnocchi will sink to the bottom of the pan. When they return to the surface, remove them with a slotted spoon, drain and serve with melted herb butter and the grated Parmesan.

Paella

I have included this Portuguese version of the dish because we have been used to eating it when on holiday there. It is thought to be a fish dish but in truth there is as much, if not more, meat in it than fish. As it is rice based, however, I decided to include it in this section. Paella is best cooked in large quantities and shared as a family meal. Almost any shellfish can be used and the Portuguese add any peas, beans and fresh herbs they may have available in the garden.

To serve 4

2 small chickens or 1 large one, cut into 8 pieces

1 lb baby squid, cut into rings and steamed

1 lb cooked prawns

12 mussels, steamed with the squid until they open

1 lb pork, diced

2 onions, chopped

4 garlic cloves, chopped

4 tomatoes, skinned and halved

3 green peppers, sliced lengthways

2 red pimentos

1 lb rice

1/2 cup olive oil

1 cup cooked peas and/or green beans

2 tsp. turmeric powder

Salt & pepper

Fish stock

Method

Chop the chickens into eight pieces, brown in the oil in a large pot, remove and set aside. (In Portugal the pot they use looks rather like a wok without the long handle, just two small metal handles at each side to lift it from the cooker.) Add the pork and brown. Add the squid, onions, garlic, tomatoes, turmeric and peppers and stir fry for a few minutes more. Add the browned chicken, rice and fish stock, season and simmer gently until the rice is cooked. Scatter the shellfish and peas over the top and give the whole a gentle stir. Serve as it is, in the pot in which it was cooked.

Thai Fried Noodles
(Pad Thai)

Pad Thai is Thailand's national dish. It is made with a special type of dried noodle called Sen Lek, a medium flat rice noodle about $1/10$ inch wide. It can be cooked in seconds but it pays to have all the ingredients ready in advance.

To serve 4 – 6

4 tbsp. vegetable oil

3 garlic cloves, finely chopped

1 egg

4 oz. dry sen lek noodles, soaked until soft and drained

2 tbsp. fish sauce

2 tbsp. lemon juice

1 tsp. sugar

3 tbsp. dried shrimp, ground or chopped

$1/2$ tsp. chilli powder

3 tbsp. peanuts, ground or pounded

2 tbsp. chopped chi po (preserved turnip)

2 oz. tinned or fresh beansprouts, washed and drained

2 spring onions, sliced into rings

Bunch of coriander leaves

Method

Heat the oil in a wok or frying pan and fry the garlic until golden. Break the egg into the pan and stir for a couple of seconds so that it forms threads. Add the noodles and stir-fry to ensure they mix well with the garlic and egg. In turn, add the lemon juice, fish sauce, sugar, half the peanuts, the shrimp, chilli powder, beansprouts, spring onion and chi po stirring all the time. When the noodles are soft, turn the lot out into a serving plate and spread the remaining peanuts and coriander over the top. Serve immediately.

West Country Pies

In 1790, Parson Hawker of Morwenstow wrote about a pie he had been served at a feast in Cornwall. He said at first he was offered rye bread 'as wheat is unknown in Cornwall' and last came 'a huge and mysterious pie, a hillock of brown dough that reeked like a small volcano with steaming puffs of savoury vapour when the massive crust which lay like a tombstone over the mighty dish was broken conger eels, pilchards and oysters were mingled piecemeal, their intervals slushed with melted butter and clotted cream'.

In 1875, Sabine Baring-Gould described a West Country favourite of his known as 'Squab Pie'. It was originally made from young pigeons taken from a culverhouse or dovecote. In his day, the pies consisted of a mix of "mutton, veal, bacon, apple, onion, pepper and salt, and a pilchard or two, Devonshire cream and occasionally, newly fledged young rooks, which were still highly relished", all under a crust.

Another Cornish delicacy was 'Stargazy pie', a piecrust through which the heads of pilchards gazed skywards. It has been said of the Cornish that "The Devil never dared cross the Tamar or he would verily been put under a crust!"

CHAPTER NINE

BARBECUE

We use a gas-fired barbecue all year-round and in the winter our neighbours are often amused to see us cooking under an umbrella in all weathers. Every 'Fat Boy' knows all about cooking on a barbecue so I have no intention of going into detail about how and what to cook. Here, however, are a few ideas to try. Yet again, it is the fun of experimentation that is the secret. I will not get involved in the debate as to which barbecuing system is the best. Wood, gas or charcoal all have their good points but when you get down to it – it is the marinade that makes the meal.

Stuffed Grilled Squid

The ideal way to cook these little devils is on the hot plate of a barbecue, with a glass of chilled New Zealand chardonnay in your hand.

To serve 4 – 6

12 small squid (frozen ones from your local supermarket, filleted and cleaned)

3 slices plain white bread

1 onion, finely chopped

2 slices smoked rindless bacon, chopped into tiny cubes

1 garlic clove, chopped fine

1 tbsp. Thai fish sauce

1 tbsp. dark soy sauce

4–5 anchovy fillets, finely chopped

$1/2$ tsp. freshly ground nutmeg

1 egg

1 tsp. hot chilli sauce

Juice from half a lemon

Salt & pepper

12 wooden toothpicks

Method

Defrost the squid and separate the tentacles from the body of the fish. Chop the tentacles into small pieces and set aside. Remove any fins on the body, chop and add to the tentacles. Fry the bacon in a little butter and when nearly cooked, add the onion and continue to fry until softened. Add the squid tentacles and garlic and stir-fry for a few seconds more, then remove from the heat and place in a bowl to cool. Discard the crust then chop the bread finely and add to the bowl, together with all remaining ingredients. Add salt and pepper to taste and mix well. Place the stuffing in the fridge for half an hour or so to allow the flavours to blend. Stuff the squid with the mixture and pin the opening with a toothpick to hold the stuffing in place. On the hot plate of a barbecue, or in a frying pan on a cooker, spread a little oil and fry the squid for about 4 or 5 minutes, turning occasionally. Do not overcook.

Remove the toothpicks and serve as a starter, with a squeeze of lemon and a green salad.

Bruschetta

What mixture you choose to put on these open, grilled slices of bread can be a source of endless experimentation. I offer two that go well together. They are excellent as a nibble, when standing over the barbecue waiting for the meat to cook, the tongs in one hand and a glass of red wine nearby. Of course they also help to keep your guests happy whilst you are busy cooking.

To serve 8

1 stick of French bread

4 tomatoes, peeled, deseeded and chopped

1 large onion, finely chopped

3 cloves garlic, peeled and finely chopped

1 bunch fresh basil

1 cup black olives, stoned and finely chopped

$1/2$ cup capers, chopped

2 oz. tin anchovy fillets, finely chopped

1 fresh red chilli pepper, deseeded and finely chopped

Handful of chopped parsley

Freshly ground black pepper & sea salt

Extra virgin olive oil

Method

Mix the tomato, onion and garlic together in a bowl and drizzle on some olive oil and season with salt and pepper. Allow to stand for an hour or so. In another bowl, mix together the chopped olives, capers, anchovy fillets, chilli and the chopped parsley. Drizzle over some olive oil, season with salt and black pepper and allow to stand for at least an hour to marinate. Slice the bread diagonally into one inch thick slices, slice a garlic clove in half and rub gently on one side of the bread. Drizzle with some olive oil on both sides and place on the barbecue for a minute or two until gently browned on both sides. Spread a spoonful of the tomato mixture on half the bread slices and a spoonful or so of the olive mixture on the rest of the slices. Serve warm with a leaf or two of basil on each of the tomato slices and a parsley leaf on the olive slices.

Barbecued Leg of Lamb

This is without doubt the best way to cook new season English lamb. It will end up crispy and scorched on the outside and pink, juicy and full of flavour in the centre.

To serve 4

4–5 lb leg of lamb, boned but not rolled

Salt and pepper

Method

Cooking the lamb over an open wood fire has had the best results we have experienced. If you decide to use wood, make sure the fire has a good base of hot ash and there is enough wood on the fire to keep the heat constant. I like to put some damp stems of rosemary on the logs just before starting to cook the meat. Do not bother seasoning it at this stage, just lay it on the grill at least 4 inches above the logs, skin side down. As the fat drips from the joint, the flames will flare up and envelop it. This is quite usual. It isn't doing any harm and, after a while, the flames will die down. For a pink centre leave for 8 or 9 minutes before turning it over. Do the other side for the same length of time. If you are using a gas or charcoal barbecue light it a good 30 minutes before you need to start cooking in order to give plenty of time for the coals to heat up. Again, ensure the meat is a good 4 inches above the coals or the meat could become badly scorched. Remove the meat from the grill, season with salt and pepper and allow it to rest for a good 10 minutes under a sheet of tinfoil. Carve and serve with chutney, (see page 133) a mixed green salad and either couscous or a potato cake.

Sosaties

A South African braaivleis or barbecue speciality introduced, no doubt, by the South East Asian slaves imported into South Africa by the Dutch in the 17th century. There are many variations of this recipe and South African families adapt it to suit their particular taste.

To serve 4 – 6

3 lbs lean lamb, cut into 2 inch chunks

1 clove garlic

4 medium onions – 2 quartered, 2 thinly sliced

3 tbsp. soft brown sugar

$1/2$ pt. milk

Lamb or beef dripping

6 fl oz. fresh lime juice or undiluted lime juice cordial

2 tbsp. hot curry powder

1 dried red chilli, finely chopped

$1/2$ tsp. whole cloves

1 cup white wine vinegar

1 tbsp. flour (optional)

1 big knob of butter

Method

Slice the garlic clove and rub the cut sides around the inside of a plastic or earthenware bowl and leave the sliced clove in the bowl. Put in the meat and cover with the milk and sugar. Fry the sliced onions in the dripping until well browned, add the curry powder, lime juice, cloves, chilli and vinegar and seasoning and fry for 1 minute, stirring all the time. Add the fried onion mixture to the bowl and stir well. Leave, covered in the fridge overnight or longer. When ready to cook, lift the chunks of lamb from the bowl with a slotted spoon and thread the quartered onions and the meat onto skewers. Put the marinade mixture into a saucepan with the flour and butter and bring to the boil. Simmer until reduced and check the seasoning. The sauce should be fairly thick and spicy. Place the skewers on the barbecue and grill, turning regularly, until cooked. Serve with the sauce, yellow rice, chutney and a green salad.

Espetada de Vaca

Described simply as barbecued beef, this might appear a rather dull recipe but, in fact, this method of barbecuing meat on Madeira is mouth-wateringly delicious and simple to prepare.

To serve 4

6 inch piece of fillet of beef (cut from the thick end of the fillet)

10 cloves garlic

Sea salt

Butter

Olive oil

4 x 12 inch skewers of mature bay or metal meat skewers

Method

Discard any sinew or excess fat from the fillet and cut into at least 16 equal sized chunks. Marinade the meat for a couple of hours or longer, with a rub made with 4 fresh chopped bay leaves, 5 cloves of the garlic, finely chopped, a good sprinkle of sea salt and a drizzle of olive oil. When ready to cook, thread the meat onto the bay or metal skewers and cook slowly on the barbecue (oak or apple wood barbecue would be ideal) without allowing the meat to burn. Melt the butter in a ramekin, squeeze the remaining garlic into the butter and season with salt. When the meat is cooked, place a skewer on each plate and brush the meat thoroughly with the garlic butter. In Madeira the 'espetada' is suspended, dripping in butter and garlic, from a special metal stand in the centre of the table with a small saucer under to collect the drips. Serve with a green salad and a chunk of freshly baked homemade bread.

Barbecued Spare Ribs

Serves 4 as a starter or 2 as a main course

1 lb pork spare ribs, cut into 3 inch lengths

1 tbsp. each soy sauce, white wine vinegar, tomato puree and honey

2 cups chicken stock (made with stock cube, if necessary)

2 tbsp. tomato ketchup

Salt & pepper

Method

Place the ribs in a large pan of salted water and bring to the boil. Simmer on low heat for about an hour until the ribs are almost cooked through, but before the meat starts falling off the bone. Remove from the heat and drain.

Mix together the soy sauce, vinegar, ketchup, tomato puree, honey and stock and bring to the boil. Lay the ribs neatly in an ovenproof ceramic dish large enough to contain them. Season the sauce and pour over the ribs. Leave in the fridge for several hours, basting from time to time. This is best done the day before. When about to cook, put the dish in the oven for a few moments to allow the marinade to run. Remove the ribs and grill them on the barbecue until cooked through. In the winter or when it is too wet to barbecue, fry the ribs in a little oil until well browned, transfer them to an oven dish and finish them in the oven until cooked. Reduce the marinade by at least a half by boiling rapidly until it becomes thick and glutinous. Pour the marinade over the ribs and serve. The result should be finger-licking good but you will need bowls of water to wash your hands afterwards!

Barbecued Fillet of Pork

This recipe is based on a Spanish tapas dish and is good as a starter for a barbecue meal.

To serve 4 as a starter

1 lb pork fillet, trimmed

1 level tsp. each of cumin seeds, coriander seeds and fennel seeds, roughly ground

1 tsp. turmeric powder dissolved in 3 tablespoons of hot water

4 garlic cloves, crushed to a paste with rock salt

1 tsp. paprika or cayenne pepper if preferred

1 tbsp. olive oil

1 tbsp. red wine vinegar

Salt & freshly ground black pepper

Method

Cut the pork fillet in half lengthways and then into 1 inch cubes. Hammer the cubes flat between two pieces of clingfilm until they are no more than $1/4$ inch thick. Place the meat in a small mixing bowl, sprinkle with the dried spice seeds and the rest of the ingredients and mix with your hands until the meat is well coated. Cover and leave in the fridge overnight, or for as long as possible, to allow the spices to infuse. When you are ready to cook, thread the meat onto 4 skewers (if you are using wood skewers make sure they are well soaked in water) and either grill on a barbecue or a griddle pan on a hot plate of an oven. They should take no more than 2 or 3 minutes on each side, season with salt and freshly ground black pepper and serve on a few salad leaves with a glass of dry sherry.

Barbecued Chicken Thighs

I came up with the idea of cooking chicken thighs using three different marinades when I couldn't make up my mind which one to choose. The result is far more exciting than the chicken thighs themselves deserve!

To serve 8

24 boned chicken thighs (they come in packs of 12 in supermarkets)

Soya & ginger marinade

3 tbsp. dark soy sauce

2 tbsp. mirrin

1 inch ginger, grated

Lemon & garlic marinade

Juice of 2 lemons

4 cloves garlic, crushed

Salt & pepper

1 onion, finely sliced.

1 tbsp. olive oil

Spice marinade

1 level tsp. each of cumin seeds, coriander seeds and fennel seeds, roughly ground

1 tsp. turmeric powder, dissolved in 3 tbsp. of warm water

4 garlic cloves, crushed to a paste with rock salt

1 tsp. paprika

1 tbsp. red wine vinegar

1 tbsp. olive oil

Method

Prepare the marinades in separate bowls. Skin the chicken thighs and place 8 in each of the bowls, covered by the marinade and leave to infuse as long as possible or overnight. When you are about to start barbecuing, thread the thighs, one from each bowl in turn, onto 8 skewers (metal if possible, if using wood, ensure they are first soaked in water) and grill on the barbecue for 3 or 4 minutes on each side. Serve with a salad of your choice.

"It is perhaps surprising to realise that English and continental cookery draw on a common tradition. The first English cookery book, Form of Cury, attributed to the cooks of Richard II, is from the same period as Viandier by Taillevent. The French words boudin, pudding, bacon, rosbif and bifteck all have English origins... British cookery is basically medieval, as shown by the predominance of cereals in foodstuffs, the sweet-and-sour contrasts and the traditions of a large breakfast and of cheese as a dessert... As so many dishes are served with boiled vegetables which have a rather bland flavour, they are often enlivened with a variety of sauces and condiments, often quite spicy: chutneys, curry, Worcestershire and Cumberland sauces, anchovy sauce, and butter sauce. This habit dates back to the Indian influence in the period of the British Empire... British cookery today is simple and unpretentious, but with the high quality of indigenous ingredients that need no more than simple cooking, the cuisine is in a class of its own..."

Larousse Gastronomique

CHAPTER TEN

VEGGIE STUFF

Although I have no time for the aggressive vegetarian, I accept that there are many dishes made exclusively with vegetables which are delicious. The one most popular with the family over the years has been the nut roast which, when produced at my daughter's annual summer party, tends to be consumed very quickly and not just by the vegetarians. Apart from the nut roast, I have chosen to include ways of preparing vegetables that will go with most of the dishes described earlier.

The potato has for years been treated with suspicion since it was introduced to regal culinary recipes by King James in 1619 and indeed it was outlawed in south-west France in 1630 as a cause of leprosy. Today, however, it has been both a fad food adopted by some and treated as poison by those protein only dieters. Nowhere has the potato been more highly prized, as a food staple, than in Ireland.

Broad Bean Salad

We grow two or three different varieties of broad bean each year in order to try and extend the season as much as possible. The truth is, however, as soon as the beans begin to plump up and before they are truly ready, we start picking them. Young, bright-green, fresh broad beans are, without doubt, our favourite summer vegetable. We eat them lightly boiled with a knob of butter and loads of salt and pepper, 'a l'Anglaise', as the French say. The broad bean was cultivated by ancient civilizations and originated in Persia and Africa. This cold salad is delicious made with young beans or skinned mature ones.

To serve 6

2 lbs fresh broad beans

8 rindless rashers of back bacon

4 hard-boiled eggs

1 2 oz. tin anchovy fillets

Olive oil, salt, pepper and lemon juice for the dressing

Handful of chopped parsley

Method

Fry the bacon until crisp and set aside on kitchen paper to drain. When cool, chop into $1/2$ inch pieces. Shell the beans and cook them in boiling water for only a few minutes until they are just tender, drain and refresh them in cold water. Skin the beans, if necessary. Lay them in a serving dish and sprinkle with the chopped bacon. Shell and chop the eggs and scatter over the bacon. Lay the anchovy fillets across the top, make the dressing and drizzle over. Serve immediately when still warm or store, covered, in the fridge until required.

Couscous

Couscous refers to the semolina grain from which it is made as well as a series of North African dishes, soups and stews. Nowadays it comes processed and pre-cooked and is simple to prepare. I have, however, chosen to include a few variations and some suggestions for side dishes. Couscous can be served as an alternative to rice or mashed potato and is perfect when eaten with fish or meatballs.

To serve 6

1 lb dried couscous

1 pint of boiling water

1 tsp. salt

3 tbsp. virgin olive oil

Method

Put the dried couscous in a bowl and pour the boiling water over it, stirring so that the water becomes absorbed evenly. Allow to stand for 10 minutes until the couscous has plumped up and then stir in the salt and olive oil. Break up any lumps that appear and keep covered until all trace of water has been absorbed.

Variations

To serve coloured couscous, add $1/2$ tsp. of powdered saffron or turmeric to the water before pouring it over the grain.

Pile the couscous in the centre of a large plate and serve with pitted dates and raisins to form a pattern, scattered over and around the pyramid shape.

Side dishes served with couscous

Fry 4 thinly sliced large onions in olive oil until they are very brown. Add 2 tsp. of honey, $1/2$ cup of raisins and 1 tsp. powdered cinnamon. Stir on low heat for a few moments and serve in a small dish.

Bring a 1 lb mixture of broad beans and frozen peas to the boil in salted water and simmer until just cooked. Add a sprinkling of currants and lashings of butter, season and serve as a side dish with a bowl of yoghurt.

Stuffed Aubergine

To serve 4

2 large aubergines

1 2 oz. tin anchovy fillets

2 slices bread, crusts removed

2 fl. oz. milk

2 cloves garlic, finely chopped

$1/2$ tbsp. powdered cumin

1 tbsp. dried basil

4 oz. raisins, soaked for a while in water

1 oz. breadcrumbs

8 oz. grated strong Cheddar cheese

Olive oil for frying

Salt and freshly ground black pepper

Method

Slice the aubergine lengthways and, with a sharp knife, score the flesh deeply in the centre and around the edge, being careful not to pierce the skin. Sprinkle the flesh of each half with salt and leave for half an hour to draw out any bitter taste. Rinse under cold water, drain and dry with a paper towel. Heat the olive oil in a frying pan and fry the aubergine, flesh side down, for about 20 minutes until the flesh can be easily removed.

Gently scoop out the flesh leaving the skin of the aubergine intact. Soak the slices of bread in the milk and squeeze dry. Chop the anchovy fillets and mix well with the garlic, cheese, spices, raisins and soaked bread. Fry the mixture in a little of the oil for a minute or two and then stuff each of the aubergine skins. Lay the stuffed vegetables in a shallow, oiled baking dish, sprinkle with breadcrumbs and bake for about 30 minutes until the top is lightly browned. Serve hot with a dollop of butter on each portion.

Variation

Instead of a stuffing of bread, anchovy fillets and milk, fry a chopped onion in oil until golden, add 1 lb minced lamb, the chopped garlic, salt and pepper and fry until the meat changes colour. Add 2 oz. pine nuts and a tablespoon of tomato concentrate. Stuff the aubergine skins with the meat stuffing and place them in a shallow dish and bake as above. If the stuffing seems too dry, mix in $1/2$ tin of skinned tomatoes, finely chopped.

Marianne's Nut Roast

This is an ideal dish for a summer lunch and will satisfy 'Fat boy' meat eaters as much as veggies – I promise! It is quick to make and uses simple ingredients and the fun is you can play with your own variations.

To serve 4 – 6

1 oz. butter

1 onion chopped

8 oz. selection of mixed nuts to include cashew, walnuts and peanuts

3 garlic cloves, finely chopped

1 tsp. mixed dried herbs

2 slices wholemeal bread

2 tsp. yeast extract or a large dollop of Marmite

1/2 pint vegetable stock, made with a cube if necessary

Salt and pepper

Method

Sauté the chopped onion in the butter until it becomes translucent and then add the garlic and stir for a few more minutes. Place the nuts and bread in a mincer and grind well. Bring the stock and yeast extract or Marmite to the boil and remove from the heat. Add the nut mixture, herbs and onions to the stock and season with the salt and pepper. Stir the mixture, which should be fairly loose and pour it into a greased 1 lb loaf tin. Bake in a hot oven for about 30 minutes until well browned and allow to cool. Turn out onto a dish, slice into portions and serve hot or cold. You could vary this recipe by adding cheese or sundried tomatoes, but I don't think you can beat the basic formula.

Stuffed Onions

This is an Arab recipe I found recently. It makes a delicious starter or accompaniment for any meat dish. The Arabs tend to make them with lamb, but we prefer to use minced beef.

To serve 4 or more

2 large onions

1 lb minced beef

3 tbsp. lemon juice or 2 tbsp. tamarind paste

2 tbsp. parsley, finely chopped

2 tsp. ground cinnamon

1 tbsp. sugar

1/2 tsp. allspice

1 tbsp. tomato concentrate

3 tbsp. vegetable oil

Salt & pepper

Method

Cut off the top and bottom of the onion and peel carefully. Make a cut from the centre to the side of both onions, from top to bottom. Boil for about 15 minutes until the onions soften and start to open up. Detach each layer carefully and leave to cool. Mix the minced meat, cinnamon, tomato concentrate, parsley and allspice together and season well. Put a tablespoon or so of the mixture in the centre of each onion leaf and gently roll up tightly. Place any discarded onion bits in the bottom of an ovenproof dish and lay the onion parcels close together on them. Pour over a 1/4 pint of water with the lemon juice, sugar and oil mixed. Simmer gently until they are tender and most of the water has been absorbed. When cooked, remove from the oven, sprinkle some sugar over and place under the grill for a minute or two to caramelise. Serve hot or cold.

Stuffed Cabbage Leaves

This is a meal in itself if served with boiled new potatoes. Stuffed cabbage is a common dish in Poland and Romania where they add minced pork, beef or veal or, indeed, a mixture of all three. In some parts of Romania they also stuff the cabbage with fish but I have chosen to include this veggie version which can be made as spicy as you like.

To serve 4

12 large sized cabbage leaves

8 oz. long grain brown rice

4 spring onions, chopped

1 medium sized onion

3 tbsp. oil

1 vegetable stock cube, dissolved in $1/2$ pint water or $1/2$ pint of vegetable stock

1 tbsp. dried fruit – sultanas or currants

$1/2$ tin of chopped tomatoes

1 chilli, deseeded and finely chopped

Good sized pinch each of chopped tarragon, thyme and mint

Salt and pepper

Method

Boil a pot of water and blanch the cabbage leaves for about 5 minutes. Trim the leaves, removing any tough stalks. Put the oil in a large frying pan and toss in the chopped onion. Add the rice and stir the mixture until the rice turns transparent. Add the stock, chopped herbs, dried fruit, tomatoes and chopped chilli. Season with salt and pepper and bring to the boil and simmer for 10 or 15 minutes until the rice is almost cooked and most of the liquid has been absorbed. Strain off any excess liquid and leave the mixture to cool so that it can be handled. Lay out the leaves and place a small amount of the mixture in the centre and fold the leaves around the stuffing, being careful to tuck in the sides like an envelope. Place the parcels tightly together in a casserole dish with the ends downwards. Add some of the cooking liquid to reach halfway up the parcels and place a lid on the dish. Cook gently in a slow oven for 30 or 40 minutes.

Baked Aubergine

To serve 4

3 large, firm aubergines

2 tbsp. dried oregano

4 cloves garlic, finely chopped

Olive oil

Salt and freshly ground black pepper

Method

Slice the aubergines into $1/2$ inch disks, place in a colander and sprinkle with the salt. Leave for at least an hour, longer if possible. Wash off the salt and dry the slices thoroughly on kitchen paper. Place some tinfoil on an oven tray and brush with olive oil. Sprinkle with salt and pepper, some of the chopped garlic and oregano. Lay the sliced aubergine close together on the tray and brush them with the olive oil and dust with the rest of the salt, pepper, garlic and oregano mixture. Bake in the oven for 30 minutes and then turn the slices over and cook for a further 10 minutes until they are well browned. Dribble a little olive oil over them. Serve as an accompaniment to roast meat.

Leek Tureen

To serve 4

2 lb young leeks

1/2 cup vinaigrette

1 sheet gelatine

Salt & pepper

Method

Trim the leeks and wash well. Boil in a pan of salted water for about 10 minutes until tender. Remove the leeks from the water and pat dry. Warm the vinaigrette and dissolve the gelatine in it. Line a 1 lb baking tin with clingfilm and cut the leeks to fit. Dunk them briefly in the vinaigrette and lay them side by side with ends matching. One row with white roots at the end and the next row with green tops at the end. When all the leeks are placed in the mould, cover with the clingfilm, holed with a fork to assist drainage. Cut a piece of cardboard to fit the tin. Cover it also with clingfilm and fit it into the tin. Invert the baking tin and suspend it over a couple of ramekins in a tray to catch drips. Leave in the fridge overnight to drain. When ready to serve, remove from the tin and slice into 1 inch slices. Serve with a green salad.

Roast Pepper & Aubergine Mix

To serve 4

1 aubergine, sliced

2 red peppers, sliced lengthways

1 onion, sliced

4 cloves garlic, sliced

1 or 2 tbsp. balsamic vinegar

12 black olives, halved

1 handful chopped parsley

1 handful basil

1 tbsp. capers

Salt & pepper

Olive oil for cooking

Method

Roast the sliced aubergine in olive oil in the oven until almost soft. They will absorb a lot of oil. Add the red peppers and onion and finally, the garlic and continue to roast in the oven. When roasted, add the vinegar, sliced olives, capers and herbs. Season and mix well. They can be served to accompany roast meat, barbecued steak or mixed with cold cooked pasta as a salad.

Latkes

Simple to make and distinctive in flavour, this German potato pancake can be eaten as a dish in its own right, with some fruit jelly on the side.

To serve 4

6 large potatoes, peeled

1 large onion, peeled

2 eggs

2 tbsp. flour

Salt & pepper

Butter and olive oil for cooking

Method

Grate the potatoes and strain, squeezing out as much liquid as possible. Grate the onion, mix with the potato and season. Add the flour. Beat the eggs and add to make the mixture smooth. If it is too thick add some milk; if too thin, add more flour. Heat the oil to smoking point in a large frying pan and spoon in the mixture and allow it to spread into flat circles. Cook both sides and serve.

Spicy Carrots

To serve 4

1 lb carrots peeled and sliced vertically into 2 inch long quarters

2 tbsp. white wine vinegar

2 tbsp. olive oil

2 cloves garlic, finely chopped

$1/2$ tsp. ground cumin

1 tsp. red chilli paste, diluted in 3 tbsp. of water

Salt & black pepper

Method

Boil the carrots in salted water until tender but not soft. Remove and drain. Heat the oil in a frying pan and sweat the garlic, add the remaining ingredients and bring to the boil. Add the carrots and stir continually until the juice has reduced and the carrots are well coated.

Warm Potato Salad

This makes a pleasant change from the normal cold potato salad and is quicker to produce. We prefer to use fresh tarragon but chopped parsley could be used instead.

To serve 4

6 medium sized potatoes or new potatoes if available, cleaned but in their skins

French dressing to taste

Handful of fresh tarragon, roughly chopped (dried can be used if fresh is not available)

Method

The dressing should be mixed to one's personal taste to include white wine vinegar, olive oil, mustard powder, salt and pepper and a teaspoon of sugar and half the tarragon. Boil the potatoes with the other half of the tarragon until just cooked but not flaky, remove from the water, drain and chop into 3/4 inch cubes. Pour the dressing over the warm potato, mix carefully and serve.

Champ or Colcannon

These Irish dishes are typical 'Fat boy' food and go well with stews of any kind.

To serve 4

4 lb potatoes

1/2 lb shallots or spring onions, finely chopped

8 fl. oz. full cream milk or cream

4 oz. butter

Salt & pepper

Champ

Method

Peel the potatoes, cut into quarters and boil until soft. Simmer, but do not boil, the milk and onions in a separate pot. Drain the potatoes, mash and add the milk and onion and half the butter a bit at a time until you have the right consistency. Season well and pile the champ on each plate leaving a well for the remaining butter in the centre.

Years ago, this made a complete meal for Irish farm labourers, who ate it with a spoon, dipping each mouthful into the butter.

Colcannon

Instead of shallots or spring onions boil 2 lb cabbage and follow the same instructions.

Devonshire Potato Cake

Devonians, like the Irish, tend to cook more potatoes than are required for one meal so that there are plenty left over to fry in fat or dripping or make into these delicious 'tatie cakes'. Good, solid 'Fat boy' food at its best! In Ireland, the closest dish might be called 'Boxty', which is often made with a mix of mashed and raw grated potato, baked in the oven and served with lashings of butter.

To serve 4 – 6

12 oz. cold mashed potato

Flour

6 oz. bacon, chopped into cubes

6 oz. butter

1 tsp. baking powder

Salt & pepper

Clotted cream

Method

Cut up the butter and mash into the potato. Add sufficient flour to make a firm paste, season well and stir in the bacon and baking powder. Form into a round flat cake about 1inch thick. Place on a greased baking sheet and bake in the hot oven for 30 minutes or so. Serve hot with lashings of butter or clotted cream.

Roasted Onions

To serve 4

4 white onions of equal size

Butter

Fresh thyme

Sea salt

Method

Cut a thin slice from the bottom of each onion to enable them to stand whilst cooking. Remove the outer layer of skin and cut a cross in the top of each onion to about halfway down. Press some salt into each cut with some fresh thyme and a knob of butter. Place in an ovenproof dish and bake in a hot oven for half an hour or so. Serve with a joint of meat and the rest of the vegetables.

Aubergine & Tomato Tureen

Late summer tends to be the time of year when the tomatoes in the tunnel which, I have been praying would ripen, finally turn light red. At that point, I pick them and move them inside the house to ripen fully on a windowsill. I pinched the basis of this recipe from a newspaper and altered it slightly. It requires ripe tomatoes otherwise it doesn't work. The best are, of course, the fat juicy plum tomatoes imported from Italy, which are still cheap in late summer.

Serves 6 – 8 as a starter

4 lb ripe plum tomatoes, peeled and halved lengthways

2 large courgettes

2 large aubergines

3 cloves of garlic, thinly sliced

3 sprigs fresh bush basil (the small-leaved variety)

10 fl. oz. olive oil

Extra virgin olive and balsamic vinegar for dressing

3 leaves gelatine

13 fl. oz. chicken stock or dissolve a chicken stock cube in 13 fl. oz. of boiling water

Freshly ground black pepper and sea salt

Method

Scoop out the seeds and internal flesh of the tomato halves and place them in an ovenproof dish, sprinkle with the sliced garlic, basil and olive oil, season and place in a slow oven for about half an hour or so, remove and cool. The tomatoes should still be whole but soft. Remove and drain them on kitchen paper. Strain the oil into a jug and discard the garlic and basil leaves. Top and tail the aubergines and courgettes and slice them as thinly as possible, lengthways. Heat about $1/4$ of the oil in a large pan and fry the aubergine slices in turn until cooked but before they turn brown. Aubergines absorb a vast amount of oil, so add more as required. Drain the slices on kitchen paper, being careful not to tear them. Follow with the courgette slices and drain them in the same way. When cooled season all slices well. Add the gelatine to the hot stock and stir until dissolved. Dip each slice of aubergine in the stock and line the long sides of a 2 lb loaf tin by placing the slices from the centre of the bottom of the tin, allowing them to hang over the sides. After dipping them in the stock mixture, lay a row of courgette slices on the bottom, on top of the aubergine. Follow with a layer of tomato and then a further layer of courgette and again tomato until the tin is almost overflowing. Press down gently to ensure the tin is well packed. Fold over the slices of overhanging aubergine and cover loosely with clingfilm. Stand the bread tin in a baking tin, place a weighted bread tin of equal size on top and leave to chill in the fridge overnight. When ready to serve, dip the bread tin briefly in hot water and turn out onto a serving board. Cut into thick slices and serve with a trickle of olive oil and balsamic vinegar.

Feasting

The main purpose of feasting for the Vikings and other barbarian peoples was to get drunk. The Anglo-Saxons had a broad selection of names for the feast-hall and its furnishings but most are to do with drink such as winsele (wine-hall) and ealusele (beer-hall), hardly any mention was made of the food eaten at these feasts. Toast after toast ensured that hosts and guests ended the feast happy but completely drunk. A drink, once offered, could not be refused and as a result one had to be capable of downing buckets full of drink.

from Regis Boyer La Sociabilite a table

(The tradition exists to this day in Sweden where at formal dinners, flowery toasts and long speeches are accepted as the norm).

Luncheon

It has intrigued me to discover where the word, 'luncheon', to describe the midday meal came from. 'Nunch' or 'nuncheon' occurs as early as the 14ᵗʰ century but in Johnson's Dictionary of 1755, luncheon is defined as 'as much food as ones hand can hold'. By the end of the 18ᵗʰ century, dinner, the main meal of the day, was being served later and later. By 1810, Jane Austen was referring to dinner being served at 6.30pm. As the family still breakfasted at 10.00am they must have been eager to fill the gap. In A New System of Domestic Cookery written in 1806, reference is made to 'noonings or suppers' but by 1813, when Pride and Prejudice was published, Jane refers to the Bennets making 'the nicest cold luncheon in the world'. The word by then was probably in full use to describe the cold buffet or picnic meal taken around midday.

Aphrodisiacs

Some aphrodisiacs function through analogy, like the vulva-shaped oyster or the phallic asparagus; others by association, because they remind us of something erotic... however, eating and copulating depend less on the digestive and sexual systems than on the brain. Aphrodisiacs are the bridge between gluttony and lust.

'Aphrodite' by Isabel Allende

CHAPTER ELEVEN

PUDDINGS

Well, what can I say! Every 'Fat boy' loves a pudding, especially sticky toffee and roly-poly pudding, so I have included a few other favourites as well.

It may come as something of a surprise for people to learn that the 'sugar collation', a lavish display of sugar based items not designed for eating, something new and unique, were designed for the first time in England and spread across Europe from the middle of the 16th century. The items created included model castles, animals and heraldic devices placed in the centre of the dining table, together with flowers and other table decorations. Chefs competed aggressively to produce the most spectacular displays. It was, of course, rare for anything of this nature to originate in England, even in the sixteenth century we appear to have been happy adapting and adopting ideas from abroad, mainly France and Italy. France has tended over the years to lay claim to much more than it deserves of fashionable court cuisine. On the other hand, the claim that 'haute cuisine' itself was introduced to France by the cooks brought from Italy by Catherine de' Medici on her marriage to Henry II in 1533, have long been discounted.

Marianne's Cream and Chocolate Pudding

To serve 4 – 6

4 oz. fresh white bread crumbs

2 tbsp. coffee powder

4 tbsp. chocolate powder

4 oz. demerara sugar

1/4 pt each single and double cream

Method

Mix the dry ingredients together. Lightly beat the cream and then layer the dry ingredients and cream mixture in a glass bowl, ending with a thin layer of the cream on top. Spread some grated chocolate to decorate. The pudding can be made the day before and stored in the larder.

Toffee Sticky Pudding

Before you start telling me I have the name the wrong way around, I got this particular recipe from one of my daughter's friends, whose mother is Belgian and who, he tells me, tends to get things the wrong way around all the time. Well, it's her recipe and, with thanks to her and her son, Rob Smithson, I intend to leave it the way it is. We all love puddings, especially rich, sweet, fattening ones like this. There is nothing better to finish off a meal in the winter or, indeed, at any other time of the year.

To serve 4 – 6

For the cake

2 oz. butter

6 oz. granulated sugar

1/2 lb plain flour

1 tsp. baking powder

1 egg

6 oz. stoned dates

1/2 pt boiling water

1 tsp. bicarbonate of soda

1 tsp. vanilla essence

For the sauce

4 oz. dark brown sugar

3 oz. butter

4 oz. double cream

Dressing

1 bowl of Devon clotted cream

Method

To make the cake, mix the butter and sugar together in a bowl and sift in the baking powder and flour. Beat the egg and add to the flour mixture and whisk in a blender. Chop the dates finely and lightly flour the pieces. Place the chopped dates in a pan and cover with the boiling water. Add the bicarbonate of soda and the vanilla essence and stir well. Add to the egg and flour mixture in the bowl and whisk until smooth and creamy. Place a layer of baking paper in a cake tin and fold in the mixture. Place in a medium oven for around 40 minutes or until cooked through. Just before you are ready to serve the pudding, heat the sugar, butter and double cream in a pan until it turns into a sticky, brown mixture. Remove the cake from the tin, place on a plate, cover with the sauce and place under the grill. Keep basting the cake with the sauce until it begins to congeal on top, remove from the grill and serve with lashings of clotted cream. Manna from heaven!

Traditional English Apple Pie

This is the Englishman's idea of a classic autumn pudding. It is also a good way to use up windfalls that are too damaged to join the fruit bowl. Almost any apple mix would do but the best is a mixture of cooking apples and a few pippins.

To serve 4 – 6

2 lbs apples, cored, peeled and sliced

4 tbsp. brown sugar

$1/4$ tsp. ground cloves

$1/2$ tsp. ground cinnamon

Grated rind $1/2$ lemon

Clotted cream

6 oz. plain flour

1 egg yolk

3 oz. butter (or 2 $1/4$ oz. butter and $3/4$ oz. lard)

Pinch of salt

1 $1/2$ oz. castor sugar

2 – 2 $1/2$ tbsp. iced water

Method

Sift the flour with the salt, rub in the butter and add the sugar. Mix to form a firm dough with the iced water and form into a flat disc and store, wrapped in clingfilm, in the fridge for a couple of hours. Mix the spices and grated rind together and spread the apple slices in a pie dish. Sprinkle each layer with the spice mixture and mound the fruit into a dome in the centre of the dish. Roll the pastry into a disc $1/2$ inch larger than the pie dish and shave off the extra strip, moisten and fix this strip to the edge of the dish. Moisten the strip and seal on the lid. Make a hole in the centre to release the steam. Traditionally an apple pie like this would have little ornamentation, but the pastry is often marked with a knife to form a lattice work pattern. Brush with a little water and a shake or two of castor sugar. Bake in a hot oven for 15 – 20 minutes until the pastry begins to brown then turn down the heat, cover with tinfoil and continue cooking for a further 20 minutes or so. My family always served apple pie cold with slivers of strong cheddar cheese but it is also excellent hot, with lashings of clotted cream.

Roly-Poly Pudding

Steamed suet puddings are as English as apple pie and served with the ubiquitous clotted cream, they are irresistible 'Fat boy' food.

To serve 4

1/2 lb flour

4 oz. chopped suet

1/2 tsp. baking powder

Raspberry or strawberry jam

Pinch of salt

Method

Mix the flour, suet, salt and baking powder with a little water and roll it out to a square about 1/4 inch thick. Spread it with a thick layer of jam, leaving about 1 inch all round. Wet the edges and then roll it up to form a bolster. Scald a cloth, sprinkle it with flour and then tie the sausage-shaped bolster securely in the cloth. Slide it into a fast boiling saucepan of water and boil for at least 2 hours. Ensure that the water boils constantly, as otherwise the pudding will become soggy. After 2 hours remove from the water, unravel the pudding and serve immediately with an enormous amount of clotted cream or custard and more jam. The dish can also be made with golden syrup instead of jam but the traditional pudding was always made with new season jam as a winter treat.

Spotted Dick

Another variation of the traditional old English suet pudding, this time with currants, orange zest and chopped hazelnuts. This recipe, like others in the book, can trace its lineage back to medieval England.

To serve 6

11 oz. plain flour

5 oz. shredded suet

1/2 oz. baking powder

4 oz. currants

4 oz. chopped hazelnuts

Grated zest of one orange

4 oz. sugar

4 fl oz. milk

Method

Mix all the dry ingredients together, including the fruit and add the milk to form a thick paste. Roll the mixture into a sausage-shaped cylinder. Wrap the cylinder in a tea towel, lightly dusted with flour, leaving enough space for expansion during cooking. Tie securely at both ends and place the sausage in a hot steamer for about an hour until cooked. Remove the towel and cut into slices. Serve with loads of clotted cream or custard.

Rumpot

This is the most magical alcoholic fruit syrup and it can be used all year round, to spoon over ice cream, in cakes, or as a syrup with pancakes. Any fresh fruit such as raspberries, red and blackcurrants, cherries, blueberries, blackberries, even currants, but not strawberries or tree fruit such as apples and pears, as they disintegrate.

Sugar

White rum

Method

Place the fruit, cleaned and with stalks removed, in a preserving jar and add a cup of sugar for each pint of fruit. Cover with white rum and stir gently. Avoid damaging the fruit. Cover and leave in a dark place for a month or longer. Use as required. If you put in more fruit, add sugar to the same ratio as above and top up the jar with rum.

Ratafia Cream Pudding

To serve 4

20 ratafia biscuits

2 cartons double cream

1 glass Marsala wine

1 tbsp. grated dark chocolate

Method

Crush the biscuits into the bottom of a glass bowl and cover with the Marsala wine. Whip the cream and cover the crushed biscuits. Sprinkle the grated chocolate on top of the cream and serve. Simple!

Gooseberry Pie

In mid Spring, when the gooseberry bushes are laden with a rich crop of green fruit, it is time to thin them and use the culled ones as a filling for this delicious hard crust pie.

To serve 4 – 6

1 lb gooseberries

6 oz. brown sugar

1 tsp. cornflour

1 tsp. elder-flower syrup
(if available)

$1/2$ tsp. baking powder

$1/2$ lb plain flour

4 oz. butter

3 tbsp.single cream

2 oz. castor sugar

Salt

Method

Top and tail the gooseberries. Blend the cornflour, brown sugar, the elderflower syrup and a tablespoon or so of water and add to the gooseberries in a pan. Simmer until the fruit becomes soft and mushy. Leave to cool. Should the fruit appear too runny, add a little more cornflour. Sift the plain flour, baking powder and salt into a food processor, add the butter, sugar and cream and process until it forms a malleable dough. Form into two discs of equal size and store in the fridge for an hour or so, wrapped in clingfilm. Butter a pie dish and roll out one of the discs to fit. Fill with the cool fruit mixture, ensuring it is not too runny as it would make the base very soggy. Cover with the second disc rolled to fit and pinch the edges together, moistened with a little water. Trim the surplus pastry and decorate the top as you wish with the remaining pastry, leaving a hole in the centre for steam to escape. Cook in a hot oven for 15 – 20 minutes until browned then turn down the heat and continue to cook for a further 30 minutes until the pastry is cooked through. This pie, like the apple pie, is best served warm with a great dollop of clotted cream, which melts as you eat it. It is also delicious cold with lashings of double cream or the ubiquitous clotted cream.

Syllabub

This traditional English pudding recipe is also simple to make and delicious to eat. It deserves its place as good 'Fat boy' food.

To serve 4

6 oz. castor sugar

3 tbsp. brandy

3 tbsp. dry sherry

Juice of 2 lemons (plus grated peel from both)

1 pint double cream

As much clotted cream as required

Method

Soak the grated lemon peel in the juice for a couple of hours. Strain into the sugar, stir in the brandy and sherry until well mixed and then add the cream. Beat the mixture until it holds its form when piled up. Pile it into tall glasses and chill. It tastes better made the day before it is required.

Banana & Rum Pudding

Another popular 'Fat boy' pudding which is easy to make and delicious to eat.

To serve 4

8 small bananas, peeled

4 heaped tbsp. brown sugar

1 wine glass dark rum

Juice of 1 orange

1/4 tsp. ground nutmeg

1/4 tsp. ground cinnamon

Loads of clotted cream

Method

Arrange the bananas in an ovenproof dish just large enough to hold them. Mix all the ingredients together, except the cream, and pour over the bananas. Bake in a hot oven for around 20 minutes. Serve with loads of clotted cream, which will begin to melt into the treacle sauce. Fantastic!

Chocolate and Orange Pudding

This is so rich it is almost wicked and is, without doubt, my favourite pudding.

To serve 4

8 oz. plain chocolate, broken into pieces

2 egg yolks

1 tbsp. raisins

1 tbsp. Greek yoghurt

2 tsp. grated orange peel

Method

Melt the chocolate in a bain-marie, allow to cool and then beat in the egg yolks. Fold in the yoghurt, orange peel and raisins and spoon the mixture into a 1 lb loaf tin lined with waxed paper. Chill in the fridge for 4 or 5 hours and when ready to serve, cut into slices and serve with a dollop of clotted cream.

Baklava

These are delicious and a perfect 'Fat boy' pudding or teatime treat. They're not easy to make but worth it in the end. This Middle Eastern delicacy was created as a Lenten dish by the Armenians in the 15th century. Bakh means 'Lent' in Armenian and halva, 'sweet'.

24 sheets filo pastry

1 lb sugar

1/2 pint water

2 tbsp. lemon juice

1 tsp. powdered cinnamon

5 oz. melted unsalted butter

12 oz. mix of pistachio nuts, almonds and walnuts

Method

Dissolve the sugar in the water and lemon juice and simmer until it thickens enough to coat a spoon, then allow it to cool in the fridge. Brush the bottom and sides of a large square or oblong baking dish with butter. Fit 9 of the filo sheets into the dish one at a time, brushing each with melted butter on both sides. Grind the nuts finely, shake the cinnamon powder over them and spread half the mixture on the top sheet in the dish, cover with 3 more buttered sheets then the remaining nut mixture. Place a further 6 sheets on top, one at a time, buttered as before. Cut into squares with a very sharp knife then bake in a slow oven (150°c) for 3/4 hour. Increase the oven temperature to 200°c and bake for about 15 minutes or longer, until it puffs up and turns a light golden colour. Remove from the oven and immediately pour the cold syrup over the baklava. You may decide to use less of the syrup, depending on your taste. When cold, re-cut and remove the pieces and serve.

Chocolate Mousse

This is my daughter's idea of heaven on earth and, of the several recipes we have seen for chocolate mousse, we think this the best.

To serve 4

8 oz. good quality plain dark chocolate

4 eggs, separated

9 oz. granulated sugar

2 tbsp. brandy

3 tbsp. instant coffee granules

8 tbsp. melted butter

10 fl. oz. whipping cream

Method

Melt the chocolate in a bain-marie. Beat the egg yolks with the sugar until the mixture is thick and pale yellow. Add the chocolate, then the coffee, dissolved in a drop of water, brandy and the melted butter. Whip the cream until stiff and add. Beat the egg whites into peaks and fold in. Pour the mixture into a serving bowl and leave in the fridge for a few hours before serving.

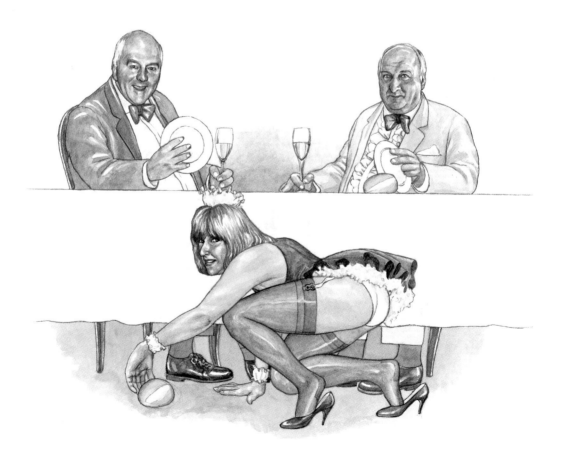

Chocolate Tart a la Michael Caines

To serve 12

For the sugar pastry (you will require a tart ring 260mm by 25mm (10" x 1"))

9 oz. plain flour

6 oz. unsalted butter

3 oz. icing sugar

2 eggs

Pinch of salt

Zest of 1 orange

For the chocolate filling

1 lb dark chocolate 40% cocoa

6 oz. milk

14 fl. oz. double cream

2 eggs

For the coffee Anglaise

17 fl. oz. milk

1 oz. milk powder

5 egg yolks

6 oz. caster sugar

4 fl. oz. double cream

1 oz. roasted coffee beans

For the crème Chantilly

10 oz. whipping cream and 1 oz. icing sugar

Method

Cream together the butter and icing sugar in a mixing bowl until white. Add the sieved flour, orange zest and salt and rub to a sandy crumble. Add the egg and mix carefully. Do not over mix. Remove from the bowl, wrap in clingfilm and refrigerate for at least 30 minutes. When you are ready to assemble the tart, roll out the pastry evenly and allow it to rest for a further 10 minutes in the fridge before attempting to line the tart ring. Place the tart ring on a flat-bottomed baking tray and line it with the pastry. Cut out a circle of greaseproof paper and place it on the pastry in the ring, fill with baking beans such as dried rice, lentils or dried beans, making sure that they are pushed into the sides. Bake in a pre-heated oven at 160°c for about 15 minutes. Remove the beans and the greaseproof paper and bake for a further 5 minutes until golden brown and then remove from the oven and allow to cool. Break the chocolate into a bowl and place over a baine-marie to melt. Break the eggs into a blender, bring the milk and cream to the boil and pour the hot creamy mixture over the eggs whilst blending. Add the creamy mixture to the melted chocolate, stirring continually. Pour the mixture into the pre-baked tart case and leave to set for 2 hours before cutting.

For the coffee Anglaise, cream together the sugar and egg yolks. Crush the coffee beans in a tea towel with a rolling pin and place them in a saucepan with the milk and cream and bring to the boil. Add about 1/3 of the creamed egg yolks and mix well. Pour the mixture back into the saucepan and, using a thermometer, cook to a temperature of 85°c, stirring continually. Pass through a sieve and allow to cool. To make the crème Chantilly sift the icing sugar into the cream and whip to a peak. To serve, simply cut the tart into 12 pieces, and serve with some coffee Anglaise and a dollop of crème Chantilly.

Coffee and Meringue Pudding

This has to be the easiest and quickest pudding to whip up for a supper party and is always much enjoyed. It is also an excellent way of using up surplus egg whites sitting around in the fridge. We usually have a tin of meringues ready in the larder for use when required but, if you need to make them fresh, use 2 oz. sugar to each egg white. Whisk the egg white until stiff and then whisk in half the sugar and fold in the rest. Drop tablespoon portions onto non-stick baking paper on a tray and bake in a slow oven for 1 – 2 hours.

To serve 6 – 8

5 oz. flaked almonds

1 tbsp. sugar

10 meringues

1/2 pint double cream

1 tbsp. Old Camp coffee

Method

Heat the almonds and sugar in a frying pan until caramelised, turning frequently, being careful not to let them burn. Allow them to cool on a piece of baking paper. Break up the meringues into a serving bowl. Whip the cream into soft peaks, mix in the Camp coffee and spoon over the crushed meringue. Scatter the almonds over the top.

Lemon Posset

Judith Pool, the owner of 'The Ring O'Bells' in Chagford, who provided this simple recipe, said "Not only does this recipe work – it is idiot proof". Well it certainly suits the 'Fat boy' idea of ease and greed! Once made and set in their individual glasses, any seasonal fruit could be added on top and served with a large dollop of clotted cream. Another idea Judith recommends is to serve the lemon cream in ramekins instead of glasses and to dust the lemon cream with icing sugar and brule with a gas gun on the day they are to be served. Repeat the dusting and brule 2 or 3 times for a real crunch factor.

To serve 6

1 1/2 pints double cream

8 oz. caster sugar

Juice of 3 lemons (Judith suggests that popping them into a microwave for 10 seconds before squeezing will produce a lot more juice, or warm in the Aga for a little longer)

Method

Bring the cream and sugar to the boil and simmer for 2 – 3 minutes. Add the lemon juice and stir until well mixed. Leave to cool slightly and then pour into individual glasses, leaving space at the top for your choice of fruit topping. Cover and refrigerate to set for a couple of hours.

Poor Knights

This recipe is known all over Europe. In France it is called pain perdu in Holland, wentelteefjes. It is an excellent way of using up stale bread and is both easy to make and a treat for the kids – they love it!

To serve 4

8 slices of stale or old bread

2 eggs

1/2 pint milk

Butter for frying

4 oz. sugar

Cinnamon or chocolate powder

Method

Whip together the milk, sugar and eggs in a soup bowl. Soak each slice of bread in turn in the mixture and fry them on both sides in the butter. Serve immediately, sprinkled with some ground cinnamon, chocolate powder or more sugar

Bread & Butter Pudding

I think it is hard to improve on this early 19th century version of a traditional English recipe for this pudding contained in Kettner's Book of the Table; however, I have also included an alternative which has become very popular recently.

To serve 4 or more

6 slices white bread, crusts removed

2 oz. butter

1 pint fresh single cream

3 oz. caster sugar

5 egg yolks and 3 egg whites

1/2 tsp. nutmeg

Method

Butter the bread slices and lay them, overlapping slightly, in an ovenproof dish. Heat the cream to boiling point, pour it over the bread and allow the dish to stand for about half an hour to soak. Beat the sugar, egg yolks and egg whites together with the nutmeg and pour onto the dish. Bake in the oven for a half an hour and serve with a little clotted cream on the side.

Alternative

Instead of the nutmeg use 1 oz. mix of sultanas and raisins. Place a drop of vanilla essence in the cream. Leave out the egg whites and butter the bread slices using unsalted butter. Scatter the dried fruit between the layers of bread and pour the warm cream over. Leave the dish to stand for 30 minutes before cooking, to allow the cream mixture to be well absorbed by the bread. Place in a bain-marie half filled with warm water and bake in the oven for 30 minutes. Don't overcook or the custard will scramble. Scatter caster sugar liberally over the top and place the dish under the grill to allow the sugar to caramelise.

Knives and Forks

Knives have been used for thousands of years as weapons or for killing, preparing and eating meat but it is only relatively recently that the knife was adapted for use at the dining table. In the Middle Ages, almost everyone carried a knife at all times and at table one was expected to use it to cut and eat food. When dining at great houses cutlery was not provided. Although forks for serving food were in use by the nobility in many European countries from the early 1100's, they appear not to have been used for eating. Thomas Coryat, in his book *'Coryat's Crudities'*, (the full name of the book is given below) published in 1611, claims he first came into contact with a fork for eating whilst travelling in Italy. (How else can one eat spaghetti? I am tempted to ask).

On his return to his home in Somerset, Coryat started using the implement at table causing much mockery and derision. His local priest even rebuked him from the pulpit for assuming God's gifts were unfit to be touched by human hands. The earliest surviving English fork is two pronged, made of silver and hallmarked 1632-3. It belonged to the Earl of Rutland and can be seen in the Victoria and Albert Museum. As forks became more common, knives no longer needed to have sharp points to spear food so were designed with a broad, rounded end on which food could also be brought to the mouth. Evidently, in North America, forks were slow to be accepted. The colonists cut their food with a knife whilst holding it down with a spoon. They then placed the knife on the table and used the spoon in the right hand to eat their meal. During the 18th and 19th centuries, knife blades began to lose their bulbous ends and started to look more like the shape we are used to today.

Thomas Coryat must have been an odd but amusing character and rates as one of the first travel and food guides. Born in 1577, the son of George Coryat, rector of Odcombe, he was educated at Oxford and entered the household of Henry, Prince of Wales. After walking to and from Venice he set off for India in 1612, again on foot, passing through Constantinople, Aleppo and Jerusalem. Having crossed the Euphrates and the Tigris he eventually reached Lahore, Agra and the Mogul's court at Ajmere. He died at Surat, in India, where he is buried.

The full name of the book he wrote in 1611 is:– *"Coryat's Crudities Hastilie gobled up in Five Moneths Travells in France, Savoy, Italy, Rhetia commonly called the Grisons country, Helvetia alias Switzerland, some parts of high Germany and the Netherlands; Newly digested in the hungrie aire of Odcombe in the county of Somerset, and now dispersed to the nourishment of the travelling members of this kingdome"*

CHAPTER TWELVE

SAVORIES

It is sad that these little treasures are fading from use – probably in light of actions by the dreaded 'diet police'. They are easy to make, delicious to eat and offer plenty of opportunity for experimentation. Before the 16th century, a feast would include four or five courses to include pottage as a starter, followed by a roast meat course then pies, which would be followed by small roast game birds, and then preserved fruits, tarts and sweet wafers. The penultimate course was the origin of our savoury dish and hence the names, Scotch woodcock and Welsh rabbit. The mention of Scotch and Welsh being an early demonstration of English political non-correctness. By the 18th and 19th centuries it was common for dinners to end with one or other of these gems as we now know them and I hope to encourage their continued use.

Anchovy & Clotted Cream

This extraordinary dish originated in Cornwall and has become one of our firm favourites. It is extremely easy to prepare and, being rather exotic, is a great hit at supper or dinner parties.

To serve 4

2 oz. tin of anchovy fillets in oil

4 slices wholemeal bread, crusts removed

1 tsp. curry powder

2 oz. butter

As much clotted cream as you wish

Method

Melt the butter in a large frying pan and fry the bread on both sides until crisp and golden. Drain the anchovy fillets, chop finely and add the curry powder. Mash the fillets with a little butter or clotted cream to form a paste and spread thinly on the fried bread. Place a dollop of clotted cream on top of each and serve immediately. Heaven!

Welsh Rabbit

The Welsh had nothing to do with this ancient English savoury dish, it was just a way of teasing the oversensitive Welsh. I have decided to offer the original, and I believe far better, 18th century version, which a friend found in an American book listing the 'delights' of English cooking.

To serve 4

4 thick slices of bread

1 glass red wine

Strong Cheddar cheese

1 level tsp. English mustard powder

Salt & pepper

Method

Toast the slices of bread and lay them on a tray. Sprinkle the wine over each slice and leave them for a minute or two on top of the stove to absorb the wine. Sprinkle the mustard powder evenly over the bread and cover each slice thickly with very thin slices of cheese. Season the cheese and place the slices under the grill until the cheese melts and turns brown. Remove and serve with Worcestershire Sauce.

Herring Roes on Toast

To serve 4

4 slices of bread

1/2 lb frozen herring roe, defrosted and with sinews removed

Plain flour

1 tsp. cayenne pepper

Butter for frying

Small handful chopped parsley

Salt and freshly ground black pepper

Method

Toast the bread, cut off the crusts and butter the slices. Season the flour well and dip the roe in to cover. Fry in the butter for a few minutes and lay on each slice of toast. Garnish with parsley and cayenne pepper.

Potted Cheddar Cheese

This recipe is an easy way of preserving and improving dry old Cheddar cheese and can be stored in the fridge for later use.

For serve 6 – 8

8 oz. old dry cheddar cheese

3 oz. unsalted butter

2 tbsp. Madeira wine (malmsey)

1 tsp. ground mace or nutmeg

Salt & pepper

Method

Finely grate the cheese and blend with the butter, Madeira and nutmeg. Season and fill a large ramekin and cover with melted butter. Serve at the end of a meal with port or Madeira.

Scotch Woodcock

To serve 4

4 slices of bread

4 eggs

1 fl. oz. cream

2 oz. butter

2 oz. tin anchovy fillets in oil

A few capers

Salt & pepper

Method

Set aside 8 anchovy fillets and mash the rest to form a paste. Toast and butter the bread with half the butter and spread thinly with the anchovy paste. Crack the eggs into a bowl, add the cream, season well and whisk. Melt the remaining butter in a heavy-bottomed pan and scramble the egg mixture until it is almost cooked but still creamy. Spoon the scrambled egg onto the buttered toast, arrange 2 anchovy fillets in the form of a cross on each portion. Scatter a few capers on top and serve.

Some Quotes

" There is nothing under the sun better for man than to eat, drink and be merry.
Go therefore, eat your bread with joy and drink your wine with cheer."

Ecclesiastes

"Give me for a beautiful sight, a neat and smart woman, heating her oven and setting her
bread! Should the bustle make the sign of labour glisten on her brow, where is the man that
would not kiss that off, rather than lick the plaster from the cheek of a duchess."

William Cobbett circa 1830

"In this competitive age, hospitality is being pressed into service and becoming an excuse
for ostentation. Dinners are given mostly by way of revenge."

William Makepeace Thackeray

"It's a very remarkable circumstance, sir, that poverty and oysters always seem
to go together."

Pickwick Papers

There was an old person of Dean
Who dined on one pea and one bean
For he said " More than that
Would make me too fat."
That cautious old person of Dean.

Edward Lear

"Where is the fool or the man of genius that is insensible to the charms of
a good dinner."

William Makepeace Thackeray

"One cannot think well, love well, sleep well, if one has not dined well."

Virginia Woolf

"The right diet directs sexual energy into the parts that matter."

Barbara Cartland

"The true gourmand never ventures out without an emetic; it is the quickest and safest way
to avoid the effects of indigestion."

Grimond de la Reyniere

CHAPTER THIRTEEN

PICKLES, CHUTNEYS & SAUCES

We consume a lot of pickle during the year and a great deal of time is spent in autumn pickling whatever we can find to add to the collection. We also make our own hot sauce from a variety of chilli peppers grown here.

Lime Pickle

Ingredients

2 lbs limes or lemons

Rough salt

1/2 pint vinegar

1 pint vegetable oil

4 tbsp. fresh ginger, finely grated

12 cloves garlic, chopped

1 tsp. fenugreek seeds, soaked in some of the vinegar

Spices

2 tsp. each of ground turmeric and ground chilli

1 tsp. each of ground cumin, coriander and fennel seeds

Fresh or dried chillies to taste

Salt

Method

Cut the fruit into quarters and sprinkle with salt. Leave in a warm room for at least 24 hours or less in the bottom of an Aga or slow oven. The objective is to allow the salt to absorb a good portion of the liquid and, eventually, the fruit will begin to look fairly dry. Mix together the fenugreek, ginger and garlic and add extra vinegar, if needed, to produce a blended puree. Wipe off the excess salt and liquid from the fruit segments and dry on kitchen paper before chopping them up into smaller bits. Put some of the oil in a heavy stainless steel pan and fry the turmeric, ground chilli, cumin, fennel and coriander for a couple of minutes before adding the puree mixture and frying for a further 2 minutes, stirring constantly. Add the remaining vinegar, the fruit and fresh or dried chillies and bring to the boil. Lower the heat and simmer for about half an hour, uncovered, until the fruit is tender. If required, add more salt or vinegar and stir gently and regularly, avoiding breaking up the fruit. When the fruit is tender, allow the mixture to cool and bottle in clean jars. The flavour should be salty, hot and tart.

Green Tomato Chutney

English chutneys are an adaptation of the original Indian ones and the name is taken from the Hindi word, 'chatni'. In India, chutney is usually a mixture of tomato, onion and other vegetables or fruit mixed with vinegar and used for one meal only. The English ones, being cooked, are designed to be kept for longer.

Ingredients

2 pints malt vinegar

1 lb demerara or other brown sugar

3 lb green tomatoes, peeled, deseeded and chopped

1 onion, chopped

1 inch fresh ginger, grated

1 tsp. each ground allspice and chilli powder

4 fresh green chillies, deseeded and finely chopped

5 oz. raisins

Salt

Method

Put all the ingredients in a large heavy saucepan (not aluminium) and simmer for about 2 hours until the mixture has thickened. Stir frequently. Cool and spoon the chutney into sterilised jars and seal when cold.

Sweet and Sour Sauce

Ingredients

8 oz. fresh or tinned pineapple juice

1 hot green pepper, thinly sliced

1 carrot, peeled and thinly sliced into matchsticks

3 tbsp. soy sauce

1 tbsp. brown sugar

3 tbsp. red wine vinegar

2 tbsp. olive oil

1 tbsp. cornflour

Method

Boil the vegetables in the pineapple juice for 10 minutes until tender. Mix the cornflour, sugar, soy sauce, oil and vinegar together and stir into the juice. Cook for a further 5 minutes or so, until the sauce thickens. Serve or store until required.

Onion Marmalade

This is excellent with cold meat. We use it as an accompaniment to the chicken breast sausage described earlier.

To store in jars

2 lb onions, finely sliced

4 tbsp. olive oil

4 oz. brown sugar

10 fl. oz. red wine vinegar

2 tsp. sea salt

1/2 tsp. chilli pepper

Method

Heat the oil in a heavy pan and fry the onions until they become translucent and begin to brown. Add all the other ingredients and simmer, uncovered, for at least 1 hour. Check seasoning and adjust to suit your taste. Continue to cook until the mixture becomes jam-like. Pour away any surplus oil, cool and store in jars until required.

Tomato Ketchup

Home-made tomato sauce is easier to make and tastier than people imagine. It can be kept in sealed bottles, either in the fridge or larder and is a great accompaniment with old meat or sausages.

To make about 1 pint

1 lb onions, finely chopped

2 lb tomatoes, peeled, deseeded chopped

8 fl. oz. white wine vinegar

3 oz. demerara sugar

2 large cloves garlic, crushed

1/2 tsp. cloves, powdered

1 red chilli, finely chopped

1 tbsp. English mustard powder

Salt & pepper

1 tbsp. olive oil

Cornflour

Method

Put the vinegar and sugar in a heavy pan and bring to a simmer. Add the tomatoes and all other ingredients except the cornflour and bring to the boil, stirring constantly. When it has reached boiling point remove to a low heat and simmer for 45 minutes or so, until soft. Check the seasoning, if it requires a little more sugar or chilli, add it now. Allow the mixture to cool a little, blitz in a blender and force it through a sieve. If the result is too runny, thicken with a little cornflour, which will also help to prevent it from separating. Pour into sterilised bottles and seal.

Bulgarian Pickled Vegetables

The best time to make this pickle is late summer when the garden is full of fresh vegetables. The fresher the vegetables are when the pickle is made, the crisper and tastier the pickle will be.

For the brine

3 pints water

4 oz. salt

1 pint white wine vinegar

For the vegetables

A selection of mixed vegetables such as carrots, cauliflowers, green, red or yellow peppers,

green beans, baby cucumbers or young swedes or turnips.

1 head dill

4 cloves garlic, peeled and split in half

3 small hot red chilli peppers

Method

Peel and cut the carrots into quarters about $2^{1}/2$ inches long. Break the cauliflower into florets. Seed and quarter the peppers. Top and tail the beans. Clean, but leave whole, the baby cucumbers and peel and cut all other vegetables into thumb sized pieces. Sterilise suitable jars and their lids in boiling water and when cool, pack neatly with a mixture of the vegetables and some of the garlic, chillies and dill in each jar. Boil the brine mixture and pour over the vegetables. Prod the pieces with a spoon or skewer to ensure that no air bubbles are trapped. Seal the jars and store for a couple of months. We like to eat them at Christmas time with cheese, game pie or other cold meats as an evening snack. Once opened, the pickles will be eaten very quickly!

Preserved Lemons

To store in jars

6 lemons

8 oz. sea salt

1 tsp. whole peppercorns

1 tsp. coriander seeds

Method

Quarter each lemon lengthways to about $1/4$ inch from the base. Mix the salt, pepper corns and coriander seeds and rub some of the mixture between the segments. Put the lemons into a glass jar with a non-metallic lid. Press them well down into the jar and add the rest of the salt mixture and top up with extra lemon juice. Ensure that, for the first week or so, the lemons are kept submerged. Store the jar in a dark, cool place for at least a month, shaking the jar from time to time. They will keep well in the brine for at least a year.

139

ACKNOWLEDGEMENTS

Many people have helped with the preparation of this book; not least those kind souls who tested each of the recipes. The 'Angels', whom are listed separately and whose support and assistance proved invaluable. Val Date, who kindly edited the book and tolerated my extraordinary spelling and grammar. Her husband, Mike, who allowed me to run off copies on his more sophisticated printer. Susan Keuls, who patiently designed and structured the book and her husband, Peter, who provided the cartoons. Last but by no means least, my wife, Marianne, who shares my enthusiasm for good and exciting food and, with the patience of the ancients, put up with the mess I created in her kitchen. She tolerated my enthusiastic search for more and more recipes and checked and rechecked what I wrote. I dedicate this little book to her with grateful thanks for years of tolerant understanding.

Jim   Jim   Michael   Andy   Jonathan   Judith

ANGELS

Their help and support in funding the printing and distribution of this book is much appreciated

Sue Taylor-Young
Christopher Little
Shirley (Pud) Cosgrave
Andrew Scott
Paul Nix
Humphrey Walters
Alex Eichhorn
Jennifer Bell
Val Date
Tony Clements

BIBLIOGRAPHY

Samuel Chamberlain, British Bouquet, (Gourmet Distributing Corp) 1963

Mary Berry, The Aga Book, (Aga-Rayburn Products Ltd)

Meg Jump, Cooking with Chillies, (The Bodley Head) 1989

Elizabeth Luard, European Peasant Cookery – The Rich Tradition, (Bantam Press 1986)

Mary Reynolds, The Love of Italian Cooking, (Octopus Books Ltd 1978)

Michael Pandya, Complete Indian Cookbook, (Hamlyn) 1980

Tony Grumley-Grennan & Michael Hardy, Gidleigh – A Dartmoor Village Past & Present,
Glebe Publishing) 2000

Rupert Croft-Cook, Exotic Food, (George Allen & Unwin) 1969

Alison Ainsworth, West Country Larder, (Peninsula Press) 1990

Claude Roden, A New Book of Middle Eastern Food, (Penguin Books) 1985

Ursula Bourne, Portuguese Cookery, (Penguin Books) 1973

Colin Spencer, British Food, an extraordinary thousand years of history, (Grub Street) 2002

Roy Strong, Feast, A History of Grand Eating, (Jonathan Cape) 2002

Thomas Coryat, Coryat's Crudities etc., 1611

CONVERSION TABLES

Weight		Volume	
Ounces	**Grams**	**Imperial**	**ml**
1/4	7	1/4 tsp.	1.25
1/2	15	1/2 tsp.	2.50
3/4	20	1 level tsp.	5
1	30	1/2 tbsp.	7.50
2	60	1 level tbsp.	15
4 oz. or 1/4 lb	110	1 fl. oz.	30
8 oz. or 1/2 lb	225	1/4 pint	140
12 oz. or 3/4 lb	340	1/2 pint	280
16 oz. or 1 lb	450	1 pint	560
14 lb or 1stone	6.5 kg	1 gallon	4.5 litres

AMERICAN CUP CONVERSIONS

1 cup equals
8 oz. or 230 grams of castor sugar
7 oz. or 200 grams of uncooked rice
5 oz. or 150 grams of cooked rice
4 oz. or 115 grams chopped onion
5 oz. or 150 grams flour

NOTES

NOTES